The Granola Cook-book

The Granola Cook-book

by Eric Melier and Jane Kaplan

arco
New York

Published by Arco Publishing Company, Inc.
219 Park Avenue South, New York, N.Y. 10003

Copyright © 1973 by Eric Meller and Jane Kaplan

Library of Congress Catalog Card Number 72-90904

ISBN 0–668–02882–3

Printed in United States of America

To
Archie, Sylvia, Kate,
Laurie, and the memory of Sidney

CONTENTS

The Granola Cook-book

By Way of Introduction

Granola used to be one of those natural or health food store curiosities—a peculiar type of cereal. You'd never find such a concoction in a supermarket. Oats and almonds and raisins and seeds and heaven knows what else. Probably very healthy, with all those real ingredients. A bit expensive; it would be easier to afford as an occasional snack than a regular breakfast. Makes a very good snack, too, with all its honey and nuts.

Times have changed, and Granola is no longer the oddity it used to be. Thousands of families across the country consume it for breakfasts and snacks with increasing frequency. Large natural food stores may offer bins of as many as six or eight varieties now, supermarkets carry one- or three-pound bags of several brands, and even many neighborhood groceries stock a variety or two. Granola is everywhere—even in the kitchen oven.

Many people have come upon a recipe somewhere and discovered how easy, fun, and inexpensive it is to make their own Granola. And many others have gone one step further to discover how natural an ingredient Granola is in cookie recipes.

It is because Granola has made its way into the home oven that *The Granola Cookbook* exists, telling in more detail than is generally known how to *make* your own Granolas, and how to *cook with* Granolas. Just as Granola is no longer the natural food curiosity, it no longer needs to be restricted to breakfasts, snacks, and cookies, nor to the few brands and varieties that are commercially available.

The first two chapters in this book have to do with Granola-making. Roughly speaking, the first gives the theory, and the second gives the recipes. The first chapter will introduce you to the few, simple steps that are involved in making Granolas, to the many ingredients that can be included, and to the considerations of flavor, nutrition, and cost that may guide you in selecting the ingredients you will use. The second chapter offers an amazing variety of Granola recipes—plain, fancy, and totally unexpected—including some unsweetened Granolas for occasional use in cooking with main ingredients that might not combine well with sweet Granola.

Incidentally, there has been some research lately that suggests Granola is no more nutritious than the supermarket's empty sugar cereals. Don't take this to heart. There are Granolas and Granolas. The ones sold in supermarkets usually are made of oats and not much else, and have relatively minimal food value. One way to judge is to *look at* the Granola and examine what you see—oats, or oats with substantial amounts of nuts, dried fruit, sesame seeds, and so on. The first chapter will tell you all about Granola nutrition, and while doing this will include recipes for especially healthful Granolas.

Chapter 3 is titled Granola for Breakfast. In it are not only many ideas and recipes, but also discussions of preparing Granola especially for children, and of how weight-watchers might approach this cereal. Having Granola for breakfast isn't necessarily just a matter of putting it in a bowl.

In Chapters 4 through 9, meat, vegetables, eggs, grains and pasta, salads, and fruit are joined with Granola. Any cookbook should have such chapters. But with Granola? We'll repeat: Granola no more needs to be confined to breakfast than it needs to be a curiosity. Nuts, oats, and raisins are conventional parts of many recipes already—it's a small and rewarding step to begin using Granola.

In Chapter 10, we're back on more familiar ground. Granola is an obviously perfect ingredient for breads. The same is true for cookies, cakes and pies, candy, and party snacks, in Chapters 11 through 14.

We hope and trust you will enjoy cooking with and making Granola. The healthy novelty may soon be a common ingredient in your kitchen. We offer you nearly 400 recipes toward that end.

As you cook, we suggest that you use natural ingredients, when available and comfortable. Especially important and easy would be to avail yourself of natural vegetable oils, whole-wheat flour, honey or molasses instead of granulated sugar, and carob powder instead of chocolate.

CHAPTER 1

MAKING GRANOLA

Granolas are widely available now. They are already made and ready for use, with raisins or almonds, honey or sugar, sesame seeds, and maybe some coconut. A few are excellent nutritionally. Some are quite fancy. And the majority are simple, processed, and fairly cheap but with not very much food value. Granolas are pre-packaged in colorful plastic at the supermarket, or are at the natural food store deep in wood or crockery bins.

So why make your own?

If you do bake your own Granola, it inevitably will be more nutritious, fresher, and less expensive. You'll have charge of what goes into it and how. And you can design it to fit your needs and whims. Indeed, you can create a constant variety of Granolas.

It might as well be asked, why bake your own bread? The Granola-making process similarly is enjoyable, increases food value, and reduces cost, and it is much easier. It will require only an hour or so of your time, with no fancy equipment, and no tricks.

Let yourself step out of the rush of the 1970's and into something down-to-earth. Forego the "packagedness" of

4

our era. Relax and let yourself get into the process of creating for yourself and your family a very real food. As you select your ingredients, be aware of all the choices available to you, and of their differing smells, textures, and appearances. Combine the various dry ingredients together, and make believe you're a child playing with grains. Really sense the sensual change that happens when the wet ingredients are mixed in. Reward yourself with the aroma that wanders from your stove and explores your kitchen.

While the cooking aroma is wafting from your oven is an excellent time to read the other chapters in this book.

BASIC GRANOLA

First, this section will strip away every possible complication, to present the simplest Granola possible, Basic Granola, the essence. That settled, the consideration of the next section will be the dozens of additions, substitutions, variations, and extravagances that can make the basic recipe into a special one that's perfect for you. The following section will review the process in more detail. Then there will be sections discussing flavor, cost, and nutrition, and how these specific concerns might well influence your choice of ingredients.

Granola: rolled oats that are spread over a cookie sheet and baked in an oven.

Before the oats are baked, a little oil and honey are combined and mixed in. The oil makes the flavor more toasty, and the honey adds a sweet temptation.

The oven temperature varies from 200° to 400° according to the maker's preference, and the time varies from 40 minutes to an hour.

Basic Granola

10 c rolled oats   ½ c vegetable oil
½ c honey

Heat the honey and oil in a saucepan over a moderate flame, stirring to blend. When thoroughly melded and fluid, add to the oats in a bowl. Mix for a minute or two, until all the oats are coated. Then spread onto an oiled cookie sheet or shallow baking pan. Place in a preheated 250° oven. It's done when lightly brown, after 40 minutes to an hour.

Note: Granola burns easily, so keep an eye on it, and stir regularly after about 20 minutes. Remove from the oven when browned, let cool, and store in a tied plastic bag for freshness. About ten servings.

If the Granola mixture is spread thinly on the cookie sheet, it will bake somewhat faster and be less apt to spill over when stirred. On the other hand, if you load the sheet, you won't have to bake several batches. We prefer to use the low temperature of 250° because burning is less apt to occur. After the first 20 minutes of baking, turn the Granola every five minutes, and be careful not to get too interested in whatever else you are doing in the meantime.

OTHER INGREDIENTS

All other Granolas are variations on the basic recipe. Simply maintain *roughly* the same number of cups of ingredients, dry and wet, with rolled or flaked grains as a substantial part, prepare these *more or less* in the manner described above, and you will be making a Granola. Don't be too cautious in taking liberties.

All or part of the *rolled oats* can be replaced by *wheat flakes, rye flakes,* or *barley flakes.* These have slightly different flavors and textures. We usually mix both rye and wheat with our oats. Wheat offers more protein than do oats, and more minerals and vitamins. (Corn flakes—flaked corn, not the commercial cereal—in our experience has been too "tooth-chippingly" hard for use.)

Once grains are milled, they oxidize quickly. It is wise to

buy only moderate amounts, use these promptly, and refrigerate them until they are used. If you do purchase larger amounts, it is possible to freeze them. Seal tightly in small plastic bags devoid of air. Mark each bag with its contents and purchase date, of course.

Granola is seldom made exclusively of flaked or rolled grains. Our handy rule of thumb—which may or may not prove valid for you—is to use oats or its substitutes for about half of the dry ingredients. And the rest? There are a world of possibilities. Here are some of them.

Another grain product and a delicious, healthy addition to Granola, is *wheat germ*. Buy it untoasted, if possible, since you'll bake it anyway, or sprinkle toasted wheat germ on at the last minute. The particular proportions characteristic of the protein enzymes in wheat germ are complementary to those in many of the other ingredients, making the total protein count for the Granola higher and more usable if wheat germ is included.*

In addition to their crunchy texture, *soy grits,* too, add good protein. *Millet,* another cereal grain, has the virtue of being low-priced as well as nutritious. Some people add *wheat flour* or *soy flour* (which should be refrigerated for storage previous to use).

Powdered milk is an excellent addition nutritionally, and it costs almost nothing. Its protein is first rate, and it is a good source of minerals, especially calcium. Close tightly and store in a cool place.

Sesame and *sunflower seeds* both contribute greatly to texture, appearance, flavor, health—and, unfortunately, expense. They are high in minerals and vitamins. And, though unbalanced in enzyme proportion, their protein is high and can be made more usable through combination with wheat germ, powdered milk, and soy grits. Sesame

---

* For more explanation of protein enzyme complementing, and of other nutritional considerations, see the Optimum Nutrition section later in this chapter.

seeds, it must be noted, are very high in saturated fatty acid, and contain less than enough linoleic acid to break it down; such ingredients require combination with others that are high in linoleic acid—such as sunflower seeds, black walnuts, and especially safflower oil. If possible, use unhulled sesame seeds, as the hulls are nutritious and also help retard spoilage.

Store unhulled sesame seeds in a tightly-closed container and keep cool and dry; hulled ones need to be refrigerated and used promptly. Sunflower seeds last longest when unshelled, of course—a factor to consider only if you have the patience to shell enough for a batch of Granola. Shelled sunflower seeds should be refrigerated in closed containers —plastic bags from which the air has been expelled are best.

Nuts add much to the character and desirability of many Granolas. The nutty flavor and texture are so appropriate amidst grains. Nuts also are high in calories, and in saturated fatty acid (especially almonds and cashews). *Black walnuts* alone have a good measure of linoleic acid, and they are the least caloric, too. *Peanuts* and *cashews* have fairly good protein, better than that of black walnuts. Peanuts have the best mineral and vitamin record, though cashews are relatively high in vitamin A. Almonds, English walnuts, macadamia nuts, and pine nuts all have enough calories to make their protein insignificant; the only things that recommend their use are flavor and fanciness, which may be enough for you. If nuts and seeds are added toward the end of the Granola's baking time, their fat will be in less danger of being altered to the unhealthy saturated form.

Like sunflower seeds, nuts keep best if they remain in their shells. If you purchase them unshelled, you can help them remain fresh by storing them in the refrigerator in a tightly closed container, especially a plastic bag. They can be frozen in plastic bags that are closed tightly and free of air.

One common Granola element that we cannot recommend is *coconut,* shredded and processed, or freshly dried. Perhaps its flavor will be enough to recommend it to you, however. It contains almost no protein, versus an abundant supply of calories. There is only a trace of linoleic acid in it to compensate for its high content of saturated fatty acids. And its offerings of minerals and vitamins are minimal. It isn't even cheap.

Like nuts, *dried fruits* are a common source of special taste in Granola. They need to be added after the baking is completed, for they burn easily and have no need of being cooked. *Raisins* are the most common, and *dried apricots* are among the healthiest. These two have equivalent calories and protein. But apricots, surprisingly, contain slightly more iron—and an immense amount of vitamin A—not to mention more potassium, niacin, and vitamin C. Many other dried fruits are readily available now— dates, apples, pineapples, prunes, bananas, currants, figs, pears. If your dried fruits are organic and untreated, store them in the refrigerator, especially in hot or humid weather; they will have a long life so long as they are cool. Most other dried fruits have been treated with sulfur dioxide so as not to mold or spoil.

Vegetable oils are high in calories and contain no protein, vitamins, or minerals. They do have saturated fatty acids, and linoleic acid, in varying combinations. The proportion in olive oil is extremely unhealthy. *Safflower, sunflower,* and *walnut oils* are among those with an excellent balance—enough, indeed, to compensate for a few other ingredients that are high in saturated fats. Of these oils, safflower is the most common, and the one we tend to use. Corn, soy, and peanut oil also have an adequate balance. When using soy oil, charring Granola is more difficult to avoid. *Sesame* oil has the advantage of remaining unsaturated even at relatively high temperatures. Keep oils tightly capped in dark bottles in the refrigerator to avoid rancidity. We must add here that if you buy the best natural food

store oils, you will have a superior ingredient, with vitamins A and E, lecithin, a natural ability to escape rancidity,
and no leftover solvents and other processing aids.

The usual *sweeteners* are *honey* and *blackstrap molasses.*
Actually, sugar is often a part of commercial Granolas;
however, it has nothing valuable to offer you, and there is
evidence that it affects body metabolism in such a way that
your body will be kept from utilizing B vitamins and calcium. Neither honey nor molasses can boast protein.
Nevertheless, molasses is only one-third as caloric as oil;
honey is one-half. And molasses is a first-rate source of
potassium, calcium, sodium, and iron. Honey provides little
of the major nutrients considered here, yet it is an excellent
source of many less noted ones. Both molasses and honey
will keep a long time. Measuring honey will be easy if you
oil your measuring cup to keep the honey from adhering.
There are a few other sweeteners with some food value,
including maple syrup, and maple, date, and brown sugars.

What else? Rice flakes, rolled wheat, wheat bran.
Squash or chia seeds. Water sometimes is added to the oil-
honey mixture. Sea salt. Carob powder, carob or chocolate
chips. Vanilla, anise, ground cinnamon or cloves. Yeast,
tiger's milk powder, or protein or lecithin powder. Coffee,
beer or apple juice, candied ginger. Soy nuts. Peppermint
tea leaves. There always will be one more possibility.

THE PROCESS

So the first step in making a Granola, if you are not
going to follow a set recipe, is to decide what you want in
it, and in what amounts. And of course, you are not obli-
gated to create your lifetime favorite mixture the first try.
Give yourself the fun of experimenting, and of learning
from coming short of the mark. And of changing. Experience is a more comfortable guide than are rules.

As you make your first estimates, it may prove helpful to
utilize an often valid, general plan, to which we have al-

ready alluded. The Basic Granola recipe used ten cups of dry ingredients (oats). Keep the same number of cups. But this time, let oats (and wheat and rye, if you like) make up half of this amount. Fill the other five cups with your choice of other dry ingredients, one or one-half cup for each. This choice might be clarified some if you think of the other dry possibilities as being of four types: powdered milk; grain products and seeds; nuts; and dried fruit. And you don't *need* to have exactly ten cups, of course. If the ingredients that you want to use, in the proportions that seem fitting, add up to eight cups or twelve—it makes little difference.

Whatever you do use, it is clever to check whether everything is on hand before you begin a batch of Granola. We once discovered at the last minute that we were out of sunflower seeds, but we decided to continue anyway. What resulted was a very dull Granola, and a realization on our part of how much we appreciate sunflower seeds.

Proceed with your chosen makings in the manner of the Basic Granola recipe. Mix the dry ingredients (except fruit) together; you might want to leave the nuts and seeds out till the end of the baking time also, so as to keep them unsaturated. In a saucepan over moderate heat, add together a half-cup of oil and about a half-cup (from one-quarter to one full cup) of honey or molasses and stir them till blended and easy to pour. Then add this liquid to the mixed dry ingredients, and stir the total for a minute or more, until all of the dry ingredients are coated. Spread on a cookie sheet or a similar baking pan, and place in a pre-heated 250° oven. After 20 minutes, begin stirring every five minutes to prevent burning and to insure an even browning. The total time will be 40 to 60 minutes—the Granola will be done when it is lightly browned. A darker brown represents the development of a carbon form which is hard to digest and causes gas. About five minutes before the Granola will be ready, sprinkle on, and mix in, the seeds and nuts (if you have left them out before). Remove the pan from the oven and sprinkle on the dried fruit. Allow to cool until the pan will not burn your hands and the Granola won't melt the plastic bag. Then store in a plastic bag that can be sealed tightly. Unless you use your Granola slowly, refrigeration is not needed, though it would insure freshness. (You can revive the flavor of an older batch by heating it in the oven at 350° for 20 minutes.) Granola can be frozen in plastic bags; defrost by letting stand at room temperature, and by "freshening" in a 350° oven for 20 minutes, if necessary.

Actually, just as Granola ingredients are variable, so is the process. Granola can be baked in a metal bowl or roasting pan, for instance. This is especially useful with very large batches. Bake for three hours at 200°, stirring every half-hour.

And the ingredients can be mixed together in varying orders, yielding different effects. If you use sea salt or date sugar, mixing these with the wet, rather than dry, ingredients will result in an individually coated, crisper, more frosted product. And adding the *dry* ingredients *to* the wet ones will bring you a crunchier, more peanut-brittle style Granola.

FLAVOR

Flavor is one obvious concern to have in mind as you plan your Granola. How do you get the combination that will best please your taste? Naturally, your answer must be a very individual one, and there is little solid direction that we can offer.

The difference created by using oats, or rye, or wheat is subtle, but it is there. Think about the breakfast cereals you ate as a child, and the breads you eat now, and you may be able to guess the effects in Granola. The surest approach would be to make a trial batch from each.

The rolled or flaked grains, being the major ingredient, determine the general grainy flavor. The influence on taste made by powdered milk, soy grits, and wheat germ in relatively small amounts is slight. They add tone. There is a sweetness to powdered milk, and a nutty bitterness in wheat germ, and perhaps a mild vegetable or bean sense to soy grits. Millet is less noticeable, for it has more of a grain taste, like that of a mild, earthy bulgar wheat. The greater the amount you use, the more influence there will be.

Whether you use honey (which is richer the darker it is) or molasses will make a big difference. The amount is important, too. One-third or one-quarter cup of sweetener affects the taste almost subconsciously, whereas a full cup makes for a noticeably sweet effect. One-half cup is an average.

The common area of most play is that of seeds, nuts, and fruits. Of the basic ingredients, these do most to add contrast and complement to the grainy flavor and to make one Granola strikingly different from another. They change markedly not only the flavor, but the appearance and texture. Little sesame seeds have an insistent flavor that shares something with nuts and grains and that is a little bitter. Sunflower seeds have a low-key, bland-nut flavor. The various nuts and fruits you surely know well already—which ones are your favorites? Which will combine for the optimal effect? How much of each will insure the desired result?

And then there is the universe of flavorings, in a universe of forms.

COST

A practical consideration that may influence your choice of Granola ingredients is that of expense. Perhaps your budget allows you only the cheapest of meals. Or you may seek to hold the line on costs generally, and yet allow yourself enough splurges to insure special interest. Which splurges require the least expenditure? Or you might desire a fancy Granola, and wonder what the charge is likely to be. Whatever your circumstances, let your mind be at rest—the price for homemade Granola is minor, especially when the ingredients are purchased wisely.

For instance, consider the Faithful Granola recipe that follows. It is not a dull mixture; nuts, fruit, and seeds are elements. It is, in fact, an average Granola. And, at the prices at which we buy our ingredients, a one-cup serving of it costs only 12¢. For that price, you could have a breakfast of 1½ organic, fertile eggs, or 3½ commercial eggs.*

Faithful Granola

3 c rolled oats	½ c sunflower seeds
2½ c rye flakes	½ c peanuts
½ c powdered milk	½ c raisins
½ c wheat germ	½ c safflower oil
½ c soy grits	½ c honey
½ c sesame seeds	

We purchase our Granola makings at two locations. Most come from a large natural food store. Others we buy at a large supermarket which is part of a giant chain. We favor large stores because they can offer lower prices, and because their fuller stocks are more apt to contain the somewhat unusual items we require. For Granola, the natural food store offers more variety than does the supermarket. Its products are healthier, too. And, most importantly for cost, it sells many grains, seeds, nuts, and oils in bulk, from giant barrels or bins or spouted canisters. The customer scoops as much as he wants of an item into a bag for purchase—or, in an ecologically helpful gesture, into his own containers brought from home and reused over and over. This is the least costly way to purchase most ingredients.

Our natural food store's grain products are less expensive than are those of our supermarket, as are its untoasted wheat germ, sesame and sunflower seeds, peanuts

---

* All costs mentioned are as of the time of writing.

and Spanish peanuts, cashews, almonds, coconut, and dried apricots. The supermarket offers a better deal on powdered milk, sea salt, raisins, apples, safflower oil, and honey. Prices of other Granola components are roughly equivalent at the two stores. Sometimes the natural food store sells broken nuts or sunflower seeds at a reduced price; the supermarket doesn't. Untoasted wheat germ at the natural store is less expensive than the toasted at either place. Rather than use the supermarket's processed commercial oil, which costs less, we purchase the natural food store's more nutritive product; however, we save about a third of the cost by buying it in bulk. On the other hand, we still use the supermarket's "instant" powdered milk, which is not only cheaper but easier to use, having been processed so as not to clump. Stores local to you may or may not have similar pricing, certainly. If your health or natural food store does not carry items in bulk, you would do well to suggest that they begin.

In our experience, rolled oats are the cheapest of the grain products used commonly in Granola. Wheat bran, and "germ and bran," are less expensive than wheat germ, if they are available to you. Spanish peanuts are the low-priced nuts. The least costly fruit is raisins, followed by currants. Safflower oil costs less than do sunflower and walnut oils. Honey bought in bulk or in five-pound cans is less expensive than when purchased in little jars, but molasses is still cheaper, though we have had difficulty in obtaining blackstrap.

Granola components available at our stores for 40¢ or less per pound include, in *increasing* order of cost: wheat bran, germ and bran, rolled oats, rolled wheat, rye flakes, wheat flakes, sea salt, soy grits, wheat germ, and barley flakes.

For 41¢ to 70¢ per pound: raisins, currants, sesame seeds, molasses, shredded coconut, dates, Spanish peanuts, sunflower seeds, powdered milk, and honey.

Costing 71¢ to $1.20 per pound: safflower oil (quart),

peanuts, figs, prunes, cashew pieces, chia seeds, and date sugar.

Available for $1.21 to $1.75 per pound: dried apples, Brazil nuts, filberts, squash seeds, dried peaches, dried pears, cashews, almonds and almond slices, walnuts, dried apricots, pumpkin seeds, and walnut oil (quarts).

And for $1.76 or more per pound: sunflower oil (quarts), pine nuts, pecans, and banana flakes.

The cheapest Granola possible would be made with rolled oats. It would include no nuts, fruits, seeds, powdered milk, soy grits, or wheat germ. The only admissible "extra" would be an even less expensive ingredient, such as wheat bran. Molasses would be preferred over honey, and less than usual oil and molasses would be used, with a little water to add compensating liquid bulk. Thus, Cheapest Granola, costing about five cents per cup:

Cheapest Granola

7 c rolled oats	¼ c molasses
3 c wheat bran	2 T water
¼ c safflower oil	

Inexpensive Granolas need not be so dull, however, so long as a few inexpensive ingredients more costly than rolled oats can be afforded. Powdered milk and especially wheat germ are not so very high-priced, and add not only to the tone of flavor but also to the nutritional value. And the least expensive nuts and dried fruits are raisins and Spanish peanuts. Add these together and you have A Good Ten-Cent Granola:

A Good Ten-Cent Granola

7 c rolled oats	1 c raisins
1 c wheat germ	½ c safflower oil
½ c powdered milk	½ c molasses
½ c Spanish peanuts	

For the sake of comparison—to show that homemade Granola really is a sanely priced food—we have created almost the most expensive Granola we could imagine. The ingredients were chosen from the price lists above, with taste a second-level concern, and nutrition a third. The result costs 38¢ per cup; if you ate meals so inexpensive three times a day, you'd be within most budgets.

Flamboyant Granola

2 c rolled oats	½ c cashews
2 c barley flakes	1 c pecans
1 c rye flakes	1 c dried pears, diced
½ c powdered milk	½ c banana flakes
½ c pine nuts	½ c sunflower oil
½ c pumpkin seeds	1 c honey

Commercial Granolas now usually cost about 18¢ per serving—and tend to be relatively plain, processed, and non-nutritive, gaining most of their attractiveness from sugar. The least expensive to come to our attention was priced at 12¢ per cup. If you wish to know the price per serving of any particular Granola, figure that one cup of most varieties will weigh one-quarter pound.

OPTIMUM NUTRITION

Arranging for maximum nutritional value in any meal is a demanding endeavor. It is especially hard with Granola, which is not only apt to contain a numerous variety of ingredients, but also must have these ingredients selected from a much greater display of possibilities. The relatively poor quality protein of oats, rye, and wheat must somehow be balanced. Another balancing act is that of linoleic acid versus saturated fatty acids—for a total of ten or 15 components, in differing amounts. What on earth will supply iron, or vitamin A, and yet not be too high in calories, sodium, or one over-balanced amino acid? Should delicious cashews be a part? Though a good protein and high in vitamin A, cashews are also a stunning source of calories and saturated fats. We have undertaken to design an optimally nutritious Granola.* Even if you don't use our recipe, the following description may give you some pointers for creating your own.

One need is to balance the amino acids that make up proteins. There are eight "essential" ones—ones that the body won't form and that therefore have to be supplied in one's diet. And at each meal, these have to be present in certain necessary proportions to each other, or else their unbalanced portions will be unusable. Of the eight, there are four which are most apt to be insufficient in a non-meat meal such as a Granola breakfast: tryptophane, lysine, isoleucine, and sulphur-containing forms.

Protein balancing is important in designing a very nutritious Granola recipe because many Granola ingredients are not well-balanced. The person eating an unbalanced Granola is taking in an unnecessary amount of unusable food; also, he may not be obtaining enough usable protein to sustain his body. According to the Food and Nutritional Board of the National Academy of Sciences, men need about 70 grams of protein daily, women need 58, boys need 60 to 85 (depending on age), girls need 55 to 62, and children need 32 to 52.

The highest protein sources for Granola are sunflower seeds, soy grits, powdered milk, peanuts, and cashews. (And, incidentally, wheat flakes are higher than are rolled oats.) Unfortunately, most of these are poorly balanced. Their full potential of protein is not available—unless the in-

---

* Most of our basic nutritional understanding and data is derived from Adelle Davis, *Let's Eat Right To Keep Fit*, Signet, 1970 (1954); Frances Lappe, *Diet for a Small Planet*, Ballantine, 1971; and Fred Rohe, "The Oil Story" and "The Sugar Story," *Organic Merchants*. We are, of course, the sole authors of the statements and calculations in this volume. Also, figures for food value and nutritional needs never do more than approximate reality, which is variable.

gredients are added in such proportions that their respective supplies of amino acids compensate for each other, resulting in an adequately balanced new combination. Daily protein needs are more easily and efficiently filled when amino acids are balanced. And when food elements are combined carefully, as in the making of a very healthy Granola, their overall protein value is raised, sometimes as much as 50 per cent, because the amino acids are better balanced in the new combination. Also, generally speaking, when you put together your own Granola, it will tend to have a higher protein value the more different kinds of ingredients you include, even if you give no time to making amino acid calculations.

People also need to consume calories; yet for many people in our culture, these seem all too easy to come by. Part of the trick nutritionally in avoiding an overabundance of calories is to eat foods that will satisfy your protein needs *efficiently*, without a high calorie count ushering the protein in. Foods containing more than 60 calories per gram of protein are suspect; many nuts do not make the grade here. Most healthy people need 2,100 to 2,500 calories per day, with teenage boys needing more, and young children and older women requiring less.

As we have mentioned before in this chapter, linoleic acid, an unsaturated fatty acid, is essential to health. It helps combat the deleterious effects of saturated fatty acids. There should always be at least an equal amount of linoleic acid to saturated fat in the foods you eat at any meal. And it is wise to limit saturated fat in the first place. Coconut, most nuts, some vegetable oils, sesame seeds, rolled oats, and milk are high in saturated fatty acids, and this fact must receive consideration in the planning of a healthy Granola. Safflower, sunflower, and walnut oils are very high in linoleic acid, and sunflower seeds and black walnuts contain smaller but helpful stores beyond what they need to counter their own saturated fats.

As for minerals, we have centered our attention on five

important ones: calcium, phosphorus, iron, sodium, and potassium. First, consider calcium and phosphorus. Besides all the needs your body has for them, they have a need for each other. Or rather, phosphorus needs calcium. If your body is to make use of the phosphorus in your Granola, it has to take in plenty of calcium, too. Your diet should contain no more than twice as much phosphorus as calcium. Adults and children need 800 mg. of calcium each day; older youngsters require 1,100 to 1,400. Molasses is an amazing source of calcium. Sesame seeds and powdered milk are good, also, and pouring fresh milk into your breakfast bowl will aid. Sunflower seeds are Granola's top supplier of phosphorus, with wheat germ a good second best, and powdered milk, sesame seeds, peanuts, and wheat flakes add helpful amounts.

People need from 8 to 15 mg. of iron every day, women and adolescents needing the higher amounts. Blackstrap molasses is again the star constituent of Granola, with sesame seeds, dried apricots, sunflower seeds, raisins, cashews, wheat germ, and soy grits providing decreasing quantities. Adding sour fruits and sweet milk to your bowl will aid in making the available iron more usable.

Sodium and potassium also need to be balanced, for they work together. Sizable amounts of both are required daily. However, our culture supplies us with much sodium, in the form of salt, so it is wisest in designing a health-oriented Granola to compensate for this fact by including no salt and by favoring potassium providers. Oats are the largest sodium source, with molasses second. The potassium providers are, first and foremost, blackstrap molasses again, plus dried apricots, soy grits, peanuts, sunflower seeds, and sesame seeds, in descending order.

With vitamins, we have given our attention again to five. Three of these are of the important B family: B_1, B_2, and niacin. It is important to realize that the B vitamins, of which there are many more than these three, are again a complicated balancing problem, more fit for a computer than a book on Granola. People need from 0.5 to 1.4 mg. of B_1, 0.8 to 1.7 mg. of B_2, and 9 to 22 mg. of niacin per day —and these three and the other B's need each other, in proportion, before they are usable. In Granola, sunflower seeds are the best B_1 ingredient, with wheat germ the runner-up. There is no good source for B_2, but wheat germ is the best available. Niacin has excellent suppliers in peanut and sunflower seeds, with wheat flakes, dried apricots, sesame seeds, and wheat germ augmenting. Milk in the Granola bowl will increase the B vitamin supply, especially B_2. Adding nutritional yeast to most Granolas will make surer your chances of receiving an adequate intake of B vitamins.

Adults and teenagers need 5,000 units of vitamin A per day, and children need half as much. Unfortunately, hardly any of the contents of Granola supply any. Cashews supply some, soy grits half as much, and sesame seeds and black walnuts half again as much. The champion source is dried apricots, without which your Granola will be devoid of vitamin A.

Last and, regrettably, least, comes vitamin C. For basic health, we need about 70 mg. per day (children need 40 to 60), and to avoid colds, of course, the requirement is very much higher. Here Granola fails us. Dried apricots and black walnuts offer slight amounts of C, as will the milk you add for breakfasts, and these are all that are available. Slicing citrus fruits into your bowl would do much toward remedying the lack.

With all these concerns in mind, we have created the recipe that follows for Optimally Nutritious Granola. With ⅔ cup of whole milk added to a serving of a little over a cup of this Granola, you will receive about half of your daily minimum need for protein. Your calorie intake will be approximately 620, a proportion of only 20:1 with the protein, and less than one-third the daily limit for all but little children and older women. The linoleic acid and saturated fatty acids are balanced. Half the daily requirement for iron is provided. The phosphorus is only one-fourth more abundant than the calcium, and the calcium supply is half the basic daily need for adults and children and one-third that for teenagers. There are roughly 1,220 mg. of potassium, seven times the amount of sodium. One-fifth to one-fourth the minimum need for vitamin A is present (and one-third to one-half the child's need). Vitamin B_1 is plentiful, at least half the basic daily need; B_2 is an adequate third; and niacin is an adequate third except for older women and younger men. The vitamin C is hardly noticeable.

Optimally Nutritious Granola

2½ c	rolled oats	½ c	peanuts
2½ c	wheat flakes	½ c	cashews
1 c	wheat germ	½ c	dried apricots,
1 c	soy grits		chopped
½ c	powdered milk	½ c	safflower oil (or
½ c	sesame seeds		sunflower, walnut)
½ c	sunflower seeds	⅔ c	blackstrap molasses
½ c	black walnuts		

Prepare these ingredients according to the method described earlier in this chapter. Since you are concerned particularly with nutrition here, be sure to purchase unhulled sesame seeds, and to seek fresh, natural, unprocessed products. Add the nuts and seeds (and wheat germ, if already toasted) near the end of the baking time to help preserve their goodness. Carefully avoid over-browning the Granola in the oven. Refrigerate each batch once it is cool enough to be poured into a plastic bag.

High-Protein Granola

Designing a Granola with a higher protein count than that of the Optimally Nutritious Granola is a challenge. Consider that oats, wheat, and rye are not high in protein, yet make up the bulk of most Granolas, and that fruit, oil, and sweetener also are not protein boosters. Wheat germ and sesame seeds, two more common ingredients, are not great providers either. Remember, too, that nuts, with high protein ratings, are apt also to have high calorie figures and poor balances of saturated fatty acids and linoleic acid. And then there is the problem of balancing the various proteins, so that the total can rise well above the sum of the parts. Beyond all this, the supply of other basic nutrients should not be left entirely to chance.

Wheat flakes have more protein than do rolled oats, so these should be used. But they would have to be utilized in a quantity far smaller than usual, creating a curiously low-grain Granola. In the High-Protein Granola mix that follows, an attempt has been made to disguise the grain-content decrease by the inclusion of a higher proportion than usual of soy grits, powdered milk, and sunflower seeds, which are all both high in protein and fairly small and unstriking. Peanuts, having the highest protein offering of any common Granola element, are an unusually major component. And dried apricots are included for the sake of their vitamin A, not to mention flavor. Wheat germ was excluded as being too low in protein, as were sesame seeds, which are also slightly high in fatty acids. Cashews and other nuts were abandoned because peanuts supply even more protein. The result is a Granola with a well-balanced protein amounting to about 37 grams for a serving of one cup plus half a cup of skim milk—well over half of the daily requirement for most people except older teenage boys.

The saturated fatty acids and linoleic acid are balanced. The calorie level is approximately 685, and the proportion to protein is 19:1, well within the 60:1 limit. About as much calcium and iron are present as with the optimal nutrition recipe. There is more phosphorus, about three-quarters the need for adults and children and one-half that for teenagers, and it is in balance with the calcium. There is slightly more potassium, and a quarter as much sodium;

obviously, these are still well within balance, and the usual American overabundance of sodium is greatly compensated for. With the increased amounts of sunflower seeds, powdered milk, and peanuts, the B vitamins have received a boost. There is one-third again as much B_1, slightly more B_2, and three times as much niacin. If the B_2 were higher yet, between two-thirds and the total of your daily B requirement would be satisfied. The offering of vitamin A is lower by one-fifth, and the vitamin C is insignificant.

High-Protein Granola

2½ c wheat flakes
1 c soy grits
1½ c powdered milk
2 c sunflower seeds
2½ c peanuts

½ c dried apricots,
    chopped
½ c safflower oil (or
    sunflower, walnut)
½ c blackstrap molasses

LOW-CALORIE GRANOLA

Now please don't misunderstand us. Granola will never replace half a grapefruit and a tablespoon of cottage cheese, if the lowest calories possible are your goal. However, if you love Granolas and want to make one that is *relatively* unfattening, that plan is in the realm of possibility. You must choose low-calorie ingredients, and abjure high-calorie ones. You must also keep the calories within the balance of utilizability to the protein.

Rolled oats have fewer calories than do wheat flakes. Molasses has fewer than does honey. Seeds and nuts, oil and sweetener, are high calorically. Especially low are oats and powdered milk. Other ingredients are in the middle; thus, even though they are not high, their inclusion would raise the total. In the Low-Calorie Granola recipe included below, oats and powdered milk are the featured ingredients. The molasses and oil are used in notably slight quantities, and water is included to help stretch the moist ingredients;

this Granola will be less sweet than most. Small amounts of sunflower seeds and dried apricots are introduced for the sake of nutrition and flavor.

A cup of this Granola, served with one-half cup of skim milk, yields around 320 calories, about half that of Optimally Nutritious Granola and of High-Protein Granola. The ratio to its protein is a satisfactory 23:1. In most respects, the nutritional value of Low-Calorie Granola is inferior; vitamin-mineral pills after breakfast might be in order. Its protein is sufficient in amount for children, but not for adults. It offers less than half the potassium of the other two recipes, and several times the sodium; nevertheless, its potassium still outweighs its sodium. The iron and calcium contents are sufficient to slightly low. There is only slightly more phosphorus than calcium. The vitamin A is equivalent to that present in the high-protein mix, as is the vitamin C. There is half as much of vitamins B_1 and B_2 as there is in the optimal nutrition Granola, and less than one-third as much niacin. With Granola, significantly reducing calories goes hand-in-hand with reducing nutrition.

Incidentally, the calories in this recipe can be reduced still further, to 300, if apple juice replaces the skim milk. The protein is also reduced still further, unfortunately; the new ratio to calories is 30:1, still well within bounds. There is more iron, potassium, and vitamin A, and less of calcium, phosphorus, and B vitamins. The saturated fatty acids are also reduced.

Low-Calorie Granola

7 c rolled oats	⅓ c blackstrap molasses
1 c powdered milk	¼ c safflower oil (or
⅓ c sunflower seeds	sunflower, walnut)
½ c dried apricots, chopped	2 T water

The topic of Granola and weight-watching will be further discussed in a section in Chapter 3, the Granola for Breakfast chapter.

CHAPTER 2

RECIPES FOR GRANOLA

So now, if you have read the first chapter, you know the ins and outs of making Granola. If you have not read it, we suggest that you do before you explore the present one, especially the sections titled "Basic Granola" and "The Process," which explain generally how Granola is prepared. This information will be important for you here, since the recipes in this chapter are based on that background knowledge. Many are only lists of ingredients, with preparation instructions included when they are special.

The 55 Granola recipes in this chapter have been categorized for your convenience. The first section is General Recipes. These Granolas are fundamental ones, with the common makings and proportions; the simplest and most typical are placed first. The second sequence contains Granolas that emphasize particular ingredients—Feature Recipes. Fancy Recipes follow—those that are especially unusual, sweet, generous, or striking. And the fourth grouping is Unsweetened Recipes. When it comes to using Granolas in, for instance, vegetable dishes, these unsweetened varieties sometimes may be the most appropriate, and several of them also would make excellent party snacks.

Tropical Granola? Read on.

GENERAL RECIPES

Vanilla Granola

6 c   rolled oats
1 c   wheat germ
1 c   sesame seeds
1 c   sunflower seeds

1 T   vanilla extract
½ c   vegetable oil
½ c   honey

Novice's Cereal

3 c   rolled oats
1 c   soy grits
⅔ c   almonds, chopped

1 t   sea salt
¼ c   vegetable oil
¼ c   molasses

Nursery School Granola

3 c   rolled oats
¼ c   wheat germ
½ c   shredded coconut
½ c   sunflower seeds

¼ c   butter
⅓ c   honey
¼ c   water

Wheat and Rye Granola

3 c   wheat flakes
3 c   rye flakes
1 c   wheat germ
1 c   sesame seeds

1 c   peanuts
1 c   raisins
½ c   vegetable oil
½ c   molasses

Leslie's Favorite

6 c   rolled oats
2½ c   rolled wheat
2 c   wheat germ
½ c   sunflower seeds
½ c   sesame seeds

2 c   nuts (any kind)
2 c   shredded coconut
1 c   vegetable oil
2 c   honey or brown sugar
    (or combination)

Linda's Granola

6 c rolled oats
1½ c wheat germ
1½ c sunflower seeds
1½ c sesame seeds
 ¾ c each filberts and
         almonds, chopped

2 c shredded coconut
2 t vanilla extract
¾ c vegetable oil
1½ c honey

After the baking is over, stir in any dry fruit that suits your taste.

Honest Granola

2 c rolled oats
2 c wheat germ
1 c sunflower seeds
1 c almonds
1 c cashews

⅛ t sea salt
1 t vanilla extract
1 c honey
⅔ c vegetable oil
⅔ c water

Homemade Granola

5 c rolled oats
1 c powdered milk
1 c wheat germ
1 c soy flour
1 c sunflower seeds

1 c sesame seeds
1 c almonds, chopped
1 c shredded coconut
1 c vegetable oil
1 c honey

Granola with Fruit

3 c rolled oats
2 c rye flakes
1 c powdered milk
½ c sesame seeds
½ c cashews

1 c raisins
1 c dried apricots, diced
1 c dried apples, diced
½ c vegetable oil
½ c honey

Honey-Oats Granola

2 c	rolled oats	⅛ t	sea salt
½ c	wheat germ	2 t	vanilla extract
2 T	sesame seeds	¼ c	honey
½ c	shredded coconut	½ c	brown sugar
1 T	brewer's yeast or	½ c	vegetable oil
	tiger's milk powder		

Nut-Flavored Granola

2 c	rolled oats	1 c	peanuts
2 c	wheat flakes	1 c	peanuts, ground
1 c	powdered milk	½ c	vegetable oil
1 c	soy grits	½ c	honey
1 c	cashews		

Great Sweet Granola

1 c	rolled oats	1 c	wheat berry
1 c	wheat germ	1 c	corn meal
1 c	soy grits	2 c	almonds
1 c	soy meal	2 c	raisins
1 c	buckwheat groats	3 c	honey
1 c	bran flakes		

Heat and use the honey in the regular way, as if there were oil with it.

Granola sans Oil

3 c	rolled oats	1 c	pecans, chopped
1 c	wheat flakes	¾ c	brown sugar
¾ c	wheat germ	1 t	cinnamon, ground
½ c	sesame seeds	2 t	vanilla extract

Rather than mix the vanilla in with the other ingredients, save it and sprinkle over the finished batch right after it comes from the oven.

Kristen's Granola
(A big batch of a fine basic Granola.)

7½ c	oatmeal	3 t	sea salt
1 c	wheat germ	1 c	vegetable oil
3 c	bran cereal	1½ c	brown sugar
3 c	whole-wheat flour	3 T	honey
1½ c	shredded coconut	¾ c	water
½ c	peanuts, chopped		

Dissolve salt in the liquid ingredients. Bake total mixture in a pot for three hours at 200°, stirring every 30 minutes.

FEATURE RECIPES

Granola Almond Special

3 c	rolled oats	1 c	almonds
2 c	wheat flakes	2 c	almonds, ground
1 c	wheat germ	½ c	vegetable oil
1 c	powdered milk	⅔ c	honey

Featuring Cashews

4 c	rolled oats	½ c	sunflower seeds
1 c	wheat germ	3 c	cashew bits
½ c	powdered milk	½ c	vegetable oil
½ c	sesame seeds	⅔ c	honey

Granola with Raisins

2 c	rolled oats	3 c	raisins
2 c	rye flakes	½ c	vegetable oil
1 c	powdered milk	½ c	molasses
1 c	sunflower seeds		

Seedy Granola

4 c	rolled oats	1 c	pumpkin seeds
1 c	powdered milk	1 c	pine nuts
1 c	soy grits	½ c	vegetable oil
1 c	sunflower seeds	⅔ c	honey

High-Soy Granola

2 c	rolled oats	1 c	soy nuts
2 c	wheat flakes		(roasted soybeans)
1 c	powdered milk	1 c	shredded coconut
2 c	soy grits	½ c	vegetable oil
1 c	soy flour	½ c	honey

Wheatola

4 c	wheat flakes	1 c	walnuts, chopped
2 c	wheat germ	½ c	vegetable oil
1 c	whole-wheat flour	½ c	honey
1 c	sunflower seeds		

Cereals Granola

12 c	rolled oats	1 c	walnuts, chopped
1 c	corn meal	½ c	raisins
¼ c	wheat germ	½ c	dates, chopped
½ c	soy flour	⅔ c	honey
1 c	corn flour	½ c	date sugar
½ c	sesame seeds	1⅓ c	vegetable oil
½ c	sunflower seeds, ground	1⅓ c	water

People's Cereal

4 c	rolled oats	½ c	shredded coconut
½ c	corn meal	1 t	sea salt
1 c	rice polish	1 c	honey
½ c	wheat germ	½ c	date sugar

2 c whole-wheat flour
½ c sesame seeds
2 c nuts (any kind)

1 c vegetable oil
1 c water

Granola Maple

5 c rolled oats
1 c powdered milk
1 c wheat germ
1 c sunflower seeds

1 c peanuts
1 c walnuts, chopped
½ c vegetable oil
1¼ c maple syrup

FANCY RECIPES

Munch

1½ c rolled oats
½ c wheat germ
½ c sunflower seeds
½ c sesame seeds
1 c walnuts, chopped
½ c peanuts

½ c almonds
1 c raisins
1 t cinnamon, ground
¼ c vegetable oil
¼ c honey

Mix the dry ingredients (except raisins and cinnamon) and sprinkle with the cinnamon. Bake for ten minutes, stirring regularly. Then drizzle on the oil, stir in, and the honey, and stir again. Bake again for a half-hour or so, until properly browned, stirring several times. Add the raisins.

Tropical Granola

7 c rolled oats
¾ c powdered milk
1¾ c wheat germ
1 c soy flour
1¾ c sesame seeds
1 c sunflower seeds
1 c pumpkin seeds

1½ c raisins
2 c dates, pitted and
      chopped
1½ c dried bananas,
      chopped
½ t sea salt
1¼ c vegetable oil

1 c squash seeds   ⅓ c honey
1½ c nuts (any kind)   ¼ c fruit juice
1½ c shredded coconut   (pineapple, orange)

The juice is to be added first with the oil and honey.

Pecan-Seed Crunch

5 c rolled oats   1½ c pecans, chopped
½ c wheat germ   ½ c raisins
½ c sesame seeds   ½ c vegetable oil
½ c sunflower seeds   ½ c honey
½ c pumpkin seeds   ½ c water

Shurlea's Familia

7 c rolled oats   1 c walnuts, chopped
4 c raw wheat germ   1½ c raisins
2 c soy grits   1½ c figs, chopped
1 c sunflower seeds,   1 c dates, pitted and
        chopped   chopped
2 c almonds, chopped   1 c date sugar
2 c filberts, chopped

Mix the sugar with the other ingredients and bake; there
are no wet ingredients in this recipe.

Fancy Stuff

4 c rolled oats   ¾ c currants
½ c sunflower seeds   1 c shredded coconut
⅔ c sesame seeds   ¼ c butter
¾ c cashews   ⅓ c vegetable oil
½ c almonds, slivered   ⅓ c honey

Toast almonds, sunflower seeds, and sesame seeds in a
frying pan. Then toast the cashews and coconut in the
butter. And finally, toast the oats in the oil, adding the
honey toward the end. Mix all of these and bake for 15
minutes. Add the currants.

Nutty Granola Special

3 c wheat flakes
1 c wheat germ
1 c sesame seeds
½ c walnuts, chopped
½ c hazelnuts, chopped
½ c filberts, chopped
½ c peanuts

½ c pecans, chopped
½ c cashew bits
½ c Brazil nuts, chopped
½ c almonds, chopped
1 c almonds, ground
½ c soy oil
1 c honey

For a more crunchy, chunky result, mix the dry ingredients *into* the wet ones.

Apricot Heaven Granola

2 c rolled oats
2 c rye flakes
1 c wheat germ
1 c almonds, chopped
1 c raisins

3 c dried apricots, diced
½ c apricot nectar
¼ c vegetable oil
1 c honey

The apricot nectar is mixed with the vegetable oil and honey. Refrigerate the finished Granola.

Eastern Granola
A delicacy resembling baklava in flavor.

2 c rolled oats
2 c wheat germ
1 c powdered milk
2 c sesame seeds
1 c walnuts

1 c walnuts, ground
1 c pecans, ground
1 c pistachio nuts
½ c vegetable oil
1¼ c honey

Fruity Granola

2 c rolled oats
2 c rye flakes
1 c sesame seeds
1 c raisins
1 c dried apricots, diced
1 c dried apples, diced

1 c dates, pitted and diced
½ c dried figs, diced
½ c dried pears, diced
½ c dried pineapple, diced
½ c vegetable oil
½ c honey

Coconut-Raisin Crunch

4 c rolled oats   2 c raisins
1 c powdered milk   ½ c vegetable oil
1 c soy grits   1 c honey
2 c shredded coconut

Sweet-and-Sour Granola

4 c rolled oats   1 c shredded coconut
1 c wheat germ   1 c raisins
1 c soy grits   ¾ c vinegar
1 c sunflower seeds   ¼ c vegetable oil
1 c sesame seeds   1 c honey

The vinegar is mixed with the oil and honey first.

Wispy Mint Granola

4 c wheat flakes   2 T dried mint leaves,
1 c wheat germ   crumbled (or pep-
1 c powdered milk   permint tea leaves)
2 c shredded coconut   2 t vanilla extract
2 c almonds, ground   ½ c vegetable oil
                                1 c honey

Add the mint leaves and vanilla to the oil and honey in
a saucepan. Heat over a low flame while you mix the other
ingredients.

Oriental Granola

5 c rye flakes   ¼ c raisins
1 c powdered milk   ¾ c tamari (soy sauce)
1 c rice polish   ¼ c vegetable oil
1 c soy grits   1 c honey
1 c peanuts

Mix the tamari with the oil and honey.

Carob Granola
A breakfast or a dessert?

5 c rolled oats
½ c powdered milk
½ c soy grits
1 c almond bits
1 c shredded coconut
1 c raisins

1 c carob powder (or
       cocoa powder)
1 c carob chips (or
       chocolate chips),
       optional
½ c vegetable oil
1 c honey

Mix the carob powder with the dry ingredients. Carob chips may be added after the Granola has baked. If the chips are added when Granola is still warm, they will melt; if added later, they will keep their form.

Just-Before Cereal
This is a variation, a Granola you cook over a burner, just before you serve it. Try—and enjoy.

½ c rolled oats
½ c millet
½ c buckwheat groats

½ c sunflower seeds
1 c raisins

Mix and soak overnight in water. When breakfast time approaches, bring to a boil over moderate heat. Serve with milk.

One Serving Raw

2 T rolled oats
2 T wheat germ
2 T walnuts, chopped
1 T raisins

1   apple, grated
juice of ½ lemon
2 T honey
½ c yogurt

The night before, mix the oats with ¼ cup water. Come morning, add the other ingredients for a rich and tasty single serving.

Uncooked Breakfast Mix

½ c rolled oats	2 T sesame seeds
2 T wheat germ	2 T almonds, ground
2 T sunflower seeds, ground	2 T hazelnuts, ground
	½ c dried apples, minced
2 T pumpkin seeds, ground	½ c raisins
	2 T date sugar

Mix and serve.

Uncooked Heavenly Granola

7 c rolled oats	1 c raisins
2 c wheat germ	4 bananas, sliced
2 c sunflower seeds	½ c dried apricots, chopped
1 c almonds, ground	½ c dates, pitted and chopped
½ c hazelnuts, ground	
½ c Brazil nuts, ground	

Combine and serve with apple juice. Refrigerate to store.

Uncooked Natural Mix

1 c rolled oats	1 carrot, grated
1 c hazelnuts, ground	1 c lemon juice
½ c walnuts, ground	¾ c heavy cream
¾ c raisins	¼ c honey
2 c apples, grated	2 c water
1 c bean sprouts	

Let oats sit overnight in the water. In the morning, add the other makings. Serve with yogurt. Refrigerate unused portion.

Healthy Uncooked Cereal

½ c rolled oats, pre-soaked
    in water
½ c wheat germ
1 T rice polish
2 t sunflower seeds
    ground

1 T sesame seeds
1 T chia seeds
1 T brewer's yeast
2 T date sugar

Mix and serve.

UNSWEETENED RECIPES

Basic Unsweetened Granola

6 c rolled oats
1 c wheat germ
1 c powdered milk

1 c sunflower seeds
1 c peanuts
1 c vegetable oil

Prepare this and all unsweetened Granolas in the manner of regular Granolas.

Unsweetened Nutty Granola

4 c wheat flakes
1 c wheat germ
1 c sunflower seeds
1 c black walnut pieces

1 c peanuts
1 c cashews
1 t sea salt
1 c soy oil

Unsweetened Seed Granola

2 c rolled oats
2 c wheat flakes
1 c wheat germ
1 c soy grits
1 c sunflower seeds

1 c pumpkin seeds
1 c pine nuts
1 t sea salt
1 c vegetable oil

Sesame Seed Granola—Unsweetened

Delicious as a snack, or for use in cooking. Note the double listings of quantities—the smaller amounts will yield a batch suitable for inclusion in a main dish.

3 c or 1 c wheat flakes   1 c or ⅓ c cashew bits
3 c or 1 c rye flakes   1 T or 1 t sea salt
3 c or 1 c sesame seeds   1 c or ⅓ c vegetable oil

Combine wheat and rye flakes and cashew bits. Mix oil in thoroughly. Sprinkle the salt and sesame seeds over all and mix in. Bake as usual.

Wheat Germ Granola—Unsweetened

2 c wheat flakes   ½ c sunflower seeds
2 c wheat germ   ½ c vegetable oil
½ c soy grits

Usweetened Granola with Fruit

3 c rolled oats   1 c dried apricots, chopped
2 c rye flakes   1 c dates, pitted and
½ c powdered milk   chopped
½ c wheat germ   ½ c shredded coconut
1 c raisins   1 c vegetable oil
1 c dried apples, chopped

Unsweetened Coconut Granola

One excellent use for this Granola is as a condiment for curries.

2 c rolled oats   ¼ c sunflower seeds
2 c coconut shreds   ½ c cashews
¼ c powdered milk   ½ c vegetable oil
¼ c sesame seeds

Unsweetened Herb Granola

2 c rolled oats	½ t basil, ground
1 c rye flakes	½ t oregano, ground
½ c powdered milk	½ t thyme, ground
1 c sesame seeds	1 garlic clove, minced
½ c sunflower seeds	1 t tea salt
½ t rosemary, crushed	⅓ c vegetable oil
½ t parsley, ground	⅛ c butter

In a saucepan over a low flame, combine the herbs, salt, and garlic with the oil and butter. Allow these flavors to meld over the heat while the other ingredients are mixed.

Garlic Granola—Unsweetened

Excellent as an ingredient or a party snack.

4 c rolled oats	¼ c parsley, ground
½ c powdered milk	8 small garlic cloves,
1 c wheat germ	minced or crushed
1 c sunflower seeds	¾ c vegetable oil
1 c almonds, chopped	¼ c butter
1 t sea salt	

Place the oil and butter in a saucepan over low heat, adding the garlic, salt, and parsley. Continue to heat while the other ingredients are readied.

Unsweetened Beef-Flavored Granola

A Granola especially suitable for use in meat dishes. The beef bouillon cubes can be replaced by chicken or vegetable cubes. And meat drippings or liquid consommé could be added to the vegetable oil.

1½ c rolled oats	½ c peanuts
1½ c wheat flakes	1 t sea salt
¾ c wheat germ	2 beef bouillon cubes
¾ c sunflower seeds	½ c vegetable oil

Before adding the oil to the dry ingredients, heat in saucepan over moderate flame and stir in bouillon cubes until they dissolve completely. Refrigerate final batch.

Curried Granola—Unsweetened

A zesty party snack or condiment—or use it in a vegetable or meat dish.

1½ c rolled oats	1 c shredded coconut
1½ c wheat flakes	1 c raisins
1½ c rye flakes	2 T curry powder
1 c powdered milk	2 t sea salt
1 c sunflower seeds	1 c vegetable oil
1 c peanuts	

Mix the curry powder and salt into the oil and allow to stand while the dry ingredients are being prepared.

Chili Flavored Granola—Unsweetened

4 c wheat flakes	1 c peanuts
2 c soy grits	2 t sea salt
1 c wheat germ	1 t ground pepper
1 c millet	2 T chili powder
1 c sesame seeds	1 c vegetable oil

Add the salt, pepper, and chili powder to the oil before joining with the dry ingredients.

CHAPTER 3

GRANOLA FOR BREAKFAST

The most obvious way of preparing Granola for your breakfast, naturally, is to fill a bowl with it. But which Granola? We refer you to the first and second chapters, if you have not read them already. The first of these especially will help you understand what Granola is and what range of choice is therefore available to you. It will also encourage you to create your own—one just right for you in taste, nutrition, and cost—and will guide you in the process. The second chaper proffers a full deck of specific Granola recipes, if you want to choose one ready-designed. Or the convenience of commercial Granolas might recommend itself to you, although many of these are of inferior nutritional value.

At any rate, may we suggest that you be thoughtful even about this simplest way of serving Granola? Take the time to ask your taste buds and stomach which Granola they most would favor. And find out what would please your family, too. Think about nutrition and cost as well.

You take care in selecting a casserole to prepare for dinner—why not dedicate the same care to your Breakfast Granola?

ADDING TO THE BOWL

It is usual and somehow natural to add milk to bowled breakfast Granola. We use powdered milk, prepared with water, because it is inexpensive and its ordinarily unsatisfying taste is not conspicuous amidst the more prominent Granola flavors. Perhaps *you* prefer whole milk, or even cream, or buttermilk. Be a gourmet and allow yourself what you really want. For that matter, maybe you'd really like your Granola dry, possessed of all its crunchiness. Or soaked in milk all night, and soggy.

The milk itself can be a variable. In the blender, combine milk and peanut butter, for instance, and pour that over your Granola. Or use tahini or almond butter with milk. (Another technique with the same ingredients would be to mix the peanut butter or other butter by spoon into the Granola itself, pour the milk on, and stir to blend.) Blend together milk, carob powder (or cocoa) and a little honey. Or try just milk and honey—or maple syrup, date sugar, or molasses. Other blender possibilities include vanilla or other extracts, coffee or a coffee substitute, applesauce, cinnamon and other spices, nuts, and a pitted peach or other fresh fruit.

Milk is not the only liquid possibility. Apple juice is a favorite for many people. They like its sweetness, lightness, and fruity aura. Other juices seem not to have popular followings. For a real treat, try coconut milk.

Non-liquid milk products also can be delightful, for certain palates. Yogurt, cottage cheese, or sour cream will bring you a sharp departure from the traditional Granola bowl.

In fact, how about a bowl of yogurt and *ground* Granola? Or ground Granola and just milk? The Granola as well as the liquid is a variable. The electric blender is a useful tool here. And ground Granola is another tasty and versatile food. For breakfast, it can even be used as a cooked cereal —try heating equal parts of ground Granola and milk with a bit of honey and butter in a saucepan. Or combine a lot of milk and a little Granola, powdered milk, and honey in the blender—and have a milkshake. In subsequent chapters, the ground version of Granola will be an ingredient in many a dish.

There are extra attractions that can be added to the Granola itself, stirred in before or after the milk. The most common are fresh fruits. Here you can follow the seasons, enjoying the changing variety of the ripest (and cheapest). Dried fruits are very appropriate, too, of course, as are more nuts, wheat germ, and seeds; just because you have baked a big batch of one kind of Granola doesn't mean your daily whim has to be bound by it. Or you could mix in some tiger's milk powder, lecithin, protein powder, or yeast, for extra nutrition. Maybe your sweet tooth calls for attention in the morning—add ice cream, some little red-hot candies, or a crumbled cookie or two, or even that leftover piece of cake from the night before.

Another possibility is that occasionally you really like some commercial, packaged cereal, or a bowl of mush. Go ahead, experience mixing it half-and-half with Granola.

Here's a rich dairy breakfast idea: stir in some powdered milk, malt milk, and whipped cream.

Or don't bother using a bowl at all. Use half a cantaloupe.

Breakfast Dishes

Granola-Apple Breakfast

1 c	Granola	¾ c	milk
1	apple, cored and chopped	2 T	maple syrup
		½ t	cinnamon, ground
1 c	applesauce		

Mix all ingredients together.

Granola Grapefruit

1 grapefruit	2 T honey
¼ c Granola	

Slice grapefruit in half, core it, and with a knife loosen the sections. Mix the Granola and honey and stuff this mixture between the grapefruit sections.

Millet with Granola

1 c water	½ c millet
½ t sea salt	½ c Granola
1 T butter	

Bring water with salt to boil, add butter and millet, cover, and simmer for about 20 minutes. Stir in Granola and serve.

Breakfast Salad

1 c Granola	1 banana, skinned and
½ c bean sprouts	sliced
1 apple, cored and sliced	1 c yogurt

Combine all ingredients.

Fruit, Granola, and Cream

This is an easy one to make the night before.

1 c Granola	12 dates, pitted and
¼ c lemon juice	chopped
12 prunes, pitted and	¼ c honey
chopped	⅛ t nutmeg, grated
8 figs, chopped	2 c heavy cream
	3 T date sugar

Soak Granola in lemon juice for one-half hour. Then add fruits. Heat the honey and nutmeg until fluid, and pour over Granola mixture. Cool in refrigerator for another half-hour, or overnight. Before serving, whip cream until stiff and beat in sugar. Fold the Granola mixture into the cream. If you like, serve in sundae dishes or tall glasses.

Figs and Granola with a Carrot

3 c   warm water   1 c   Granola
1   carrot, sliced   1 c   figs, chopped
3   apples, cored and sliced

In electric blender, blend water, carrot, and apples. Add this to Granola, and stir in figs.

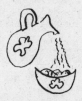

PANCAKES

Granola Pancakes

½ c   milk   2 t   baking powder
2 T   butter, melted   ½ t   sea salt
2 T   honey   ⅓ c   Granola, ground
1   egg   ¾ c   whole-wheat flour

Combine the milk, butter, honey, and egg. Stir in the baking powder, salt, Granola, and flour. Spoon batter onto oiled, hot frypan and brown on both sides.

Granola-Rice Pancakes

1 c   milk   1 T   butter, melted
¾ c   rice, cooked   ¾ c   whole-wheat flour
½ t   sea salt   ⅓ c   Granola
2   egg yolks, beaten   2   egg whites, beaten stiff

Combine the milk, rice, and salt. Mix in the yolks and butter. Then stir in the flour and Granola, and fold in the whites. Cook as usual.

Granola Potato Latkes

2 c	potatoes, grated	3	eggs, beaten
½ c	Granola	1 T	onion, grated
2 T	whole-wheat pastry	½ t	sea salt
	flour	¼ t	ground pepper

Combine the potatoes, Granola, and flour. Mix in the eggs, onion, salt, and pepper, to make a loose batter. Drop by spoonfuls onto a hot, oiled frypan and brown on both sides.

Granola Buttermilk Yeast Pancakes

1 T	yeast	1	egg, beaten
1½ c	lukewarm buttermilk	½ t	sea salt
2 T	honey	1 c	whole-wheat flour
2 T	vegetable oil	½ c	Granola

Mix yeast with ¼ cup buttermilk and the honey and leave till bubbles appear. Separately, blend oil, egg, remaining buttermilk, and salt, and mix into yeast mixture. Stir in the flour and Granola until smooth. Spoon batter onto hot, oiled pan and brown lightly on both sides.

MORE GRANOLA BREAKFASTS

As you explore further in this cookbook, you'll discover that the present chapter is not the only one with breakfast ideas. The fruit and salad chapters (8 and 9) may offer you ways you'll want to prepare fruit with Granola. The bread chapter (10) can lead you to fine toasts and rolls. And the egg chapter (6) has some very fitting recipes, too.

CHILDREN AND GRANOLA

A few months ago, we were chatting with a little boy who didn't like Granola. Most of the children of our acquaintance do like Granola, but there are also those who don't, and we were interested in finding out why. This little boy explained that Granola was not as much fun as other cereals, which, we learned, meant that it didn't come in colorful, zany boxes with prizes inside. Other children confided that Granola was too crunchy for them, or that they didn't like raisins. To our minds, none of these are unsurmountable hindrances. Granola is flexible, and if you are inventive, breakfast does not need to be a distasteful business-as-usual time.

Whether or not your child already likes Granola, fun and creative participation are what he can associate with breakfast.

First of all, Granola doesn't have to be served from a brown paper bag, or even a flimsy plastic one. Try your hand at making a container to equal those lining the super-market aisles. Cover an old cereal box or canister, for instance, with colorful contact paper pasted over with cut-outs of your child's favorite heroes. Better yet, let your child design his own Granola box, and change the design when-ever he pleases. He'll have not only a container he likes, but the pleasure of involvement, and the even greater pleasure of your support in his endeavor.

There are adventuresome ways of serving Granola, too. Some have been described earlier in this chapter. You can gently encourage and aid your child in being more aware of how he wants his breakfast—or maybe he already is aware. One approach is to have "sprinkles" available when the morning Granola is served: little bowls of extra nuts, dried fruit, coconut, wheat germ, and the like. Let each member of the family have the Granola adaptation he wants. In this, you again will be showing your child that you approve of his individuality and self-direction.

The most important thing, especially if your child doesn't like Granola, is to avoid being too suggestive or insistent. Let him have his individuality. If your child is addicted to sugared, empty commercial cereals, for example, and you would rather have him eating a substantial Granola, you can at least let him know your feelings, ask him softly what his grudge against Granola is, do a few things to make Granola more attractive to him (such as decorating a Granola canister and adding a couple of ten-cent toys to the ingredients), and then leave him space to be himself.

If there is something specific your child doesn't like about Granola, there is probably a remedy for it. Granola does not *have* to contain raisins, for example. The crunchiness can be toned down by 15-minute or overnight soaking in milk, grinding in an electric blender, or even heating the ground Granola and milk with a little honey to make a mush. A compromise that your child might appreciate would be to mix his favorite commercial cereal with Granola, half-and-half.

Another pastime children often enjoy, and receive little nutrition from, is snacking on sugar-foods. Granola is a healthy snack food, a treat for most youngsters, and hence a likely solution. When you look through Chapters 11 through 14, which include cookies, cakes, candy, and party snacks, you will probably recognize many possibilities. For that matter, in-the-house snacking might require only a bowl of Granola on the kitchen counter. And a small bag of Granola sent with your child to school or play could eliminate potato chips and candy bars.

One happy offshoot of time you spend with Granola— whether you are making a container, buying ingredients, selecting a variety, or baking a batch—is that it can be time you spend with your youngster, time in which you work together and make decisions together. Most young children are delighted to help their parents cook. And Granola is variable enough that they do not have to be relegated to merely measuring, stirring, and finding. They can help choose which ingredients will go into this batch. And you can ask them if they think one cup of sesame seeds is enough this time. They'll be learning a lot about foods and kitchens. And when the baking time comes, you can play a game of checkers or tell a story.

GRANOLA FOR WEIGHT-WATCHERS

Granola is not a weight-watcher's dream. Although its best varieties are nutritious, it is also fairly high in calories and carbohydrates. Or perhaps it *is* a weight-watcher's dream—your dream, a tantalizing one, of exactly the not-allowed food you crave. For the nutritional aspect, we refer you to Chapter 1, where you also will find a recipe for Low-Calorie Granola. As for the question of whether or not to have any in the first place, and if so, how, there are two approaches.

The first is traditional, and restriction is its watchword. You should not eat high-calorie foods at all; restrict what you eat. Or, if you really cannot go without your Granola, or whatever, restrict the quantity. Other people have fruit on their Granola in the morning. It is your solution to have a little Granola sprinkled on your fruit. As for snacking, keep the Granola out of sight. It is okay for you to cook with Granola, but be sure to look through the subsequent chapters for the recipes that contain the least Granola and other heavy ingredients. Think of the Granola you cook with as a fine spice—you add a spice by pinches, and don't eat it by the jarful. In general, make sure there is clear communication between the rational Adult and the impulsive Child in your head, so that you won't have to go through cycles of spending time first with the Child stuffing yourself with Granola, and then with the Adult wondering what happened.

A newer and more humanistic approach* says that craving comes when you deny yourself what you really want. But "really" here does not mean your urge every time you see the bag of Granola or cookies on the shelf. It means what you *really* want, that you probably have denied

---

* We are indebted to Dr. Leonard Pearson and Lilian Pearson, M.S.W., authors of *The Psychologist's Eat-Anything Diet*, Peter H. Wyden, 1973, for their stimulating ideas about food and eating.

yourself so strongly that you are not even aware of it.

Relax, take some time off. Lie down and go with the urge, see what it is, what you really want. Put aside for a few moments the should's and shouldn't's you have about food and about living. Be sensitive to your urge, and follow it where it takes you. If your urge is for Granola, for instance, then what is it about Granola that you want? Maybe it is really the fruit on top. Or the chance to sit down and rest for a while—maybe you would really prefer a shower or a nap, or a quiet, honest chat with someone. If it really is Granola you want, then keep asking what it is about Granola you want, and find out the specific ingredients that will make it perfect for you, and the setting. If you want a very nutty Granola with blueberries in it, eaten beside your sewing machine, then sneaking a few handfuls of raisin-laden Granola from a drawer in the kitchen is just not likely to satisfy you, and you'll keep eating.

Once you have gotten in touch with exactly what it is you want, then, if available, let yourself have it. And really be aware of having it, really *let* yourself have it. If it is Granola, taste it, feel it in your mouth, feel its crunch and different flavors, savor it, and feel it going down into your stomach. You're worth it. Whether or not you lose weight, you'll be a more satisfied person. And being more satisfied, more in touch, and more allowing of yourself, you just might lose weight anyway.

CHAPTER 4

MEAT DISHES, STUFFINGS, AND SAUCES WITH GRANOLA

Dishes using meats—beef, chicken, pork, lamb, and fish —are surely not the first places most people would expect to find Granola. Nevertheless, in this book we intend to demonstrate that Granola is much more broadly useful and enjoyable than most people would think. Now that we've discussed the most likely place to find Granola (breakfast), here is a chapter with Granola and meat.

In the right situations and combinations, Granola is a beneficial addition to meat. The most automatic role for it is as a substitute for such common ingredients as bread and cracker crumbs and rice. More unconcealed roles introduce its extra texture and characteristic flavor in a more manifest way, and may be great successes, or terrible flops. Most often, Granola (sometimes ground) is appropriately used as a coating for pieces of meat, as part of a topping on meat dishes, in combination with ground meat or other ingredients, or within a sauce.

The beef section in this chapter includes recipes not only for hamburgers and meat loaves, but for Stroganoff and Veal Parmesan. In the chicken section, recipes vary from a simple one in which Granola is used to coat drumsticks, to Sour Cream Chicken Livers Granola, and Granola Chicken

India. There are recipes for using Granola with pork cutlets and chops, ham, ground pork, and chunks of pork. Lamb chops, lamb curry, and even Greek Moussaka are to be found with Granola in the lamb section. And the fish used with Granola vary from salmon to swordfish, in such preparations as fried fish fillets, and Shrimp-Salmon-Granola Celebration. Ending the chapter are stuffings, sauces, and dumplings—Granola extras that will give your own meat preparations an extra touch.

BEEF

Beef Stroganoff Granola

2½ T	butter	1	onion, chopped
½ c	whole-wheat flour	½ c	mushrooms, sliced
2 c	beef stock	1 t	sea salt
1 c	sour cream	¼ t	ground pepper
1½ lbs	round steak, pounded and cut in 1 in. by 2 in. slices	1 T	parsley, ground
		½ c	Granola

Melt 1½ Tbsp. of the butter and blend in 1½ Tbsp. of the flour. When cooked to brown paste, add stock and stir till smooth. Slowly stir sour cream in and let simmer. Dredge beef in remaining flour and brown on both sides with onions and mushrooms in remaining butter. Add sauce, salt, pepper, parsley, and Granola and simmer 20 minutes.

Overseas Beef with Granola

1	onion, chopped	2 c	pot roast, cooked and diced
1	garlic clove, minced		
¼ c	bell pepper, chopped	1 c	tomato puree
¼ c	celery, chopped	¼ c	tamari
1 T	vegetable oil	¼ c	orange juice
½ t	sea salt	1 t	honey
1 t	chili powder	½ c	Granola

Sauté onion, garlic, bell pepper, and celery in oil. Add remaining ingredients except Granola and simmer 15 minutes, uncovered. Stir Granola in.

Calves' Liver Patties

1½ lbs calves' liver, ground or minced	2 eggs, beaten
2 T vegetable oil	1 t sea salt
2 onions, grated	¼ t ground pepper
¾ c cooked brown rice	¼ t marjoram, ground
¾ c Granola	¼ t thyme, ground
	6 slices bacon

Combine all ingredients except bacon. Form into six patties and wrap a slice of bacon around each, securing with toothpick if needed. Set in oiled baking pan and bake at 350° for 30 minutes.

Smothered Veal Granola-Parmesan

1½ lbs veal cutlets	½ c Granola
5 T butter	½ t sea salt
1 onion, chopped	¼ t ground pepper
1 garlic clove, minced	½ c white wine
½ c Parmesan cheese, grated	

Cook cutlets in 3 Tbsp. of the butter for ten minutes on each side. Remove veal, and sauté the onion and garlic until golden, then replace veal. Combine cheese and Granola, and cover the veal with it. Sprinkle on salt and pepper, dab on remaining butter, and pour wine over. Cover and simmer 50 minutes, checking occasionally to insure against sticking.

Veal-Granola Birds

1	onion, chopped finely	½ t	sea salt
5 T	butter	¼ t	ground pepper
¾ c	Granola	¾ c	stock
¾ c	celery, chopped finely	1	egg, beaten
½ c	hamburger	¼ c	whole-wheat flour
½ c	ground sausage	1½ lbs	veal cutlets, cut in 3 in. by 4 in. pieces and pounded
1 t	poultry seasoning	⅔ c	cream

Sauté onion in 2 Tbsp. of the butter until golden, then remove from burner. Add Granola, celery, hamburger, sausage, poultry seasoning, ⅜ tsp. of the sea salt, ⅛ tsp. of the ground pepper, ¼ cup of the stock, and egg. Mix remaining salt and pepper into flour and dredge one side of each veal piece. Divide stuffing into as many portions as there are pieces of veal, and wrap each piece around a portion of stuffing, with the dredged veal side outside. Secure with toothpicks. Sauté in 3 Tbsp. of the butter, add remaining stock and cream, and simmer for 40 minutes, covered.

Juicy Granola Hamburgers

1 lb	hamburger	¼ c	tomato sauce
1	egg, beaten	¾ t	sea salt
½ c	Granola	¼ t	ground pepper
⅓ c	powdered milk	1 t	vegetable oil

Combine all ingredients, except oil, and form into patties. Sauté in oil for 15 minutes on each side.

Oriental Granola Hamburgers

1 lb hamburger	grated ginger root)
¼ c Granola	1 egg, beaten
¼ c water chestnuts, finely diced	2 T tamari
	¼ t ground pepper
½ t ground ginger (or	1 T vegetable oil

Mix all ingredients, except oil, together and shape into large patties. In oil, sauté about 15 minutes on each side.

Granola Meatballs

1 lb hamburger	2 T molasses
1 c Granola	juice of 1 lemon
1 egg	2 T tamari
¼ c tomato juice	2 T green pepper, minced
1 t sea salt	½ c celery, minced
¼ t ground pepper	⅛ t cayenne, ground
1 c tomato sauce	

Mix hamburger, Granola, egg, tomato juice, salt, and pepper and form into balls. Stir together the remaining ingredients and heat to simmer. Put meatballs into the sauce, cover, and cook over low heat for 25 minutes.

Granola Sloppy Joes

1 lb hamburger	1 t chili powder
1 onion, chopped	1 t sea salt
1 green pepper, chopped	¼ t ground pepper
2 garlic cloves, minced	1 T parsley, ground
1 c tomato sauce	6 whole-wheat rolls, toasted
1 T tamari	
1 c Granola	

Begin sautéing hamburger in frying pan, breaking it up in the process. Add onion, green pepper, and garlic. Once meat is browned, add remaining ingredients. Simmer six minutes. Spoon over the rolls.

Tony Madrid's Meatloaf (Shrink's Meatloaf)

1 c Granola, ground	6 hardboiled eggs, shelled and diced
1½ lbs hamburger	
2 onions, diced	1 c spinach, parboiled
	¼ t tabasco sauce

Combine all ingredients and form into oiled loaf pan. Bake at 350° for 50 minutes.

Granola and Beef Blender Loaf

¼ c onion, chopped	¼ c tomato juice
¼ c celery, sliced	½ t sea salt
¼ c soybeans, soaked in water or stock	¼ t ground pepper
	½ t sage, ground
¾ c milk	1 lb hamburger
1 egg	¾ c Granola

In electric blender, blend onion, celery, soybeans, milk, egg, tomato juice, and seasonings. Mix with hamburger and Granola. Transfer to oiled loaf pan and bake at 350° for 45 minutes.

CHICKEN

Simple Granola Drumsticks

4 chicken drumsticks	¼ t ground pepper
½ c butter, melted	1 c Granola
½ t sea salt	

Dip drumsticks in butter mixed with salt and pepper, then into Granola to coat. Set in oiled baking dish and bake at 350° for 60 minutes; turn once.

Granola Chicken Breasts with Ham and Cheese

2	eggs, beaten	½ c	vegetable oil
1 t	sea salt	6	small slices ham,
¼ t	ground pepper		cooked
1	garlic clove, minced	6	slices Mozzarella
3	whole chicken		cheese
	breasts, halved	1 c	tomato sauce
1½ c	Granola	1 T	oregano, ground

Beat the eggs with salt, pepper, and garlic. Dip chicken breasts in this mixture, then in 1 cup of the Granola. Brown chicken in oil, then set into an oiled baking dish. Set a slice of ham and one of cheese over each breast. Combine tomato sauce and oregano and pour over chicken. Sprinkle with remaining Granola. Bake at 350° for 35 minutes.

Sour Cream Chicken Livers Granola

1 c	sour cream	½ t	sea salt
2	egg yolks, beaten	⅛ t	ground pepper
4	onions, sliced	1 T	paprika
4 T	butter	½ c	Granola
1 lb	chicken livers		

Heat sour cream in double boiler. Gradually add 2 Tbsp. of hot sour cream into egg yolks, beating steadily. Then slowly stir this mixture into the remaining sour cream. Simmer, stirring, until sauce is thick. Keep over hot water in double boiler. Sauté onions in butter until golden. Add livers, salt, pepper, and paprika. Cook for eight minutes. Add liver mixture, including juice, and the Granola to the sauce.

Granola Chicken India

1	frying chicken (weighing 2½ lbs), cut into pieces	1 c	celery, sliced
		1	green pepper, sliced
2 t	paprika	1½ c	uncooked brown rice
½ t	sea salt	¾ c	peanut butter
½ t	ground pepper	2 T	tamari
⅓ c	cornstarch	2 T	honey
¼ c	Granola, ground	¾ c	water
¾ c	vegetable oil	¼ c	Granola
1	onion, minced	2 c	pineapple chunks

Toss chicken pieces in mixture of paprika, salt, pepper, ground Granola, and cornstarch. Fry for 15 minutes over moderate heat in half the oil. Set chicken aside and add to skillet the onion, celery, green pepper, and rest of oil. When these have softened, stir in the rice. Separately, combine the peanut butter, tamari, honey, and water. Add peanut butter mixture, Granola, and pineapple to the rice mixture. Simmer and add chicken; cover and cook for 45 minutes, stirring several times.

Granola Baked Chicken

1	roasting chicken (weighing 3 to 4 lbs)	½ c	cashew pieces
		1 T	basil, ground
	sea salt	¼ t	ground pepper
	ground pepper	½ c	butter, melted
1	egg, beaten	3 T	honey
2 c	Granola	3 T	vegetable oil

Season the inside of the chicken with salt and pepper. Mix the egg, 1½ cups of Granola, nuts, basil, and pepper and stuff into chicken. Sew closed. Combine honey and oil and rub chicken skin with it, then sprinkle on extra Granola. Bake for 90 minutes at 350°, basting several times with pan juices and butter.

Chicken-Cream Sauté with Granola

5 green onions, chopped	⅔ c chicken stock
1 c bell pepper, chopped	⅓ c white wine
2 c cooked chicken,	1 t tarragon, ground
shredded	1 t thyme, ground
½ t sea salt	¾ c cream
¼ t ground pepper	½ c Granola
2 T whole-wheat flour	

Sauté lightly the green onions and bell pepper in 3 Tbsp. of the butter. Then stir in the chicken, salt and pepper. Reduce heat. In a saucepan, melt remaining butter, blend in flour, and add the stock, wine, and herbs. Stirring, bring to a boil. When sauce is thick, mix into chicken mixture (still over flame). Stir in the cream and Granola and serve.

PORK

Sweet-and-Sour Granola Pork Cutlets
Here Granola adds a gently exotic flavor.

1 lb pork cutlets	3 T whole-wheat flour
1 c apple juice	2 t sea salt
⅓ c wine vinegar	⅛ t ground pepper
1 c fruitless Granola	1 T honey

Marinate pork in apple juice and vinegar for half a day. Then combine ¼ cup of the marinade with the other ingredients, coat the meat with this mixture, and let dry briefly. Bake at 350° for 30 minutes, or until done.

Pork Chops with Sour Cream and Granola

3 lbs pork chops	¾ c wine
¼ c whole-wheat flour	¼ lb mushrooms, sliced
¼ lb butter	1 c sour cream
2 onions, sliced	½ c Granola

Dredge chops in flour and brown slowly in 6 Tbsp. of the butter. Add onions and cook until golden brown, then add wine; cover and simmer for 45 minutes. In remaining butter, sauté the mushrooms. Add mushrooms, sour cream, and Granola to the chops, and serve when heated.

French Granola Pork Chops

1 onion, chopped	¼ c pickle, sliced thinly
1 T pork chop grease	½ t sea salt
¼ c vinegar	¼ t ground pepper
1 t whole-wheat flour	4 pork chops, cooked
2 T consommé	and warm
2 T white wine	¼ c Granola
1 t dry mustard	

Sauté onion in pork grease for two minutes. Add vinegar and cook for two more minutes. Sprinkle with flour and add consommé and wine. When boiling, stir in mustard and simmer for ten minutes, stirring occasionally. Add pickle, salt, and pepper, and simmer for five additional minutes. Pour sauce over chops and sprinkle on Granola.

Granola Pork Loaf

1 c onions, chopped	½ t coriander, ground
1 garlic clove, minced	2 eggs, beaten
½ c butter	1 c Granola
3 c cooked pork, chopped	2 bacon strips, cooked
1½ t sea salt	and crumbled
½ t ground pepper	1 c parsley, minced
½ t cumin, ground	

Sauté onions and garlic in butter. Mix in pork, salt, pepper, cumin, and coriander, and cook for a few minutes. Add eggs, milk, ⅔ cup Granola, bacon, and parsley. Form into oiled loaf pan and sprinkle top with rest of Granola. Bake for 90 minutes at 300°.

Indonesian Pork with Granola

¼ c peanut butter	1 T cumin, ground
3 T tamari	2 T coriander, ground
1 garlic clove, crushed	2 lbs pork, cubed
¼ c Granola	vegetable oil
½ t cayenne, ground	

Mix the peanut butter, tamari, garlic, Granola, cayenne, cumin, and coriander into a paste. In a bowl, cover pork with this mixture and allow to stand 24 hours. Poke the paste-covered pork cubes onto skewers, leaving a space between each, and broil for 14 minutes on top and bottom, brushing with oil a couple of times. If there is leftover paste, heat and spread over meat for serving.

Sweet-and-Sour Pork with Granola

1 lb pork, cut into	2 T honey
1-inch cubes	2 T tamari
1 t dry sherry	4 oz sweet pickle, diced
½ t sea salt	8 oz pineapple chunks
1 T cornstarch	1 T cold water
2 c + 1 T vegetable oil	1 tomato, cut in eighths
2 garlic cloves, minced	1 c Granola
½ c vinegar	

Mix pork with sherry, salt, and 1 tsp. of the cornstarch, and let stand for 20 minutes. Deep fry pork in 2 cups of the oil at 375° for six minutes. Sauté garlic in 1 Tbsp. oil over high flame for one minute. Add vinegar, honey, and tamari to garlic. Bring mixture to boil. Add pickles and pineapple, and when mixture comes to a boil again, thicken with 1 Tbsp. cornstarch dissolved in 1 Tbsp. cold water. Add tomato and Granola, and pour over fried pork.

Baked Ham and Eggs with Granola

3 T butter	¼ c Granola
4 slices boiled ham	¼ c parsley, chopped
4 eggs	sea salt
¼ c Parmesan cheese, grated	ground pepper

Set ham slices in bottom of oiled baking dish. Break one egg onto each slice, being careful not to break the yolks. Onto each egg, sprinkle parsley, Granola, cheese, and finally salt and pepper. Dot with butter. Bake at 400° for 12 minutes.

Ham and Granola in Cream

2 onions, sliced	½ t tamari
2 T butter	2 c ham, cooked and chopped
½ lb mushrooms, sliced	1 c Granola
2 t whole-wheat flour	
¾ c cream	

Sauté onions in butter until golden brown, add mushrooms and cook four minutes. Stir in flour, cover, and simmer for five minutes. Slowly blend in cream. Then mix in the tamari and ham. When heated, stir in Granola.

Peas and Granola Over Ham

1 lb peas, shelled	4 slices ham, cooked and hot
1 onion, grated	½ c Granola
1 garlic clove, minced	
2 T butter	

In covered frypan steam peas, onion, and garlic in butter over low heat for 15 minutes. Mash and spread over ham slices. Sprinkle Granola on.

Pork and Granola Patties

½ lb	pork sausage meat	½ c	Granola, ground
1	egg, beaten	½ t	vegetable oil

Divide and shape meat into four patties, dip in egg, and roll in Granola. Fry in oil, browning well on both sides.

Southern Granola Hash

2 lbs	ground pork	1 t	sea salt
2	garlic cloves, minced	¼ t	ground pepper
3 T	butter	¼ t	rosemary
2	green peppers, diced	¼ t	thyme, ground
4	onions, diced	1¼ c	Granola
3	celery stalks, diced	1 c	Cheddar cheese,
4	tomatoes, chopped		grated

Brown pork in butter with garlic, stirring often. Add vegetables and seasonings; cover and cook slowly for 15 minutes. Stir in Granola and sprinkle cheese on. Continue to cook, covered, for another couple of minutes.

LAMB

Granola-Banana Lamb Curry

1	onion, chopped	1 t	curry powder
2	garlic cloves, minced	½ t	turmeric, ground
1 T	vegetable oil	½ t	cumin, ground
½ lb	lamb, cut in bite-sized	2	tomatoes, sliced
	pieces	3	bananas, peeled and
½ t	sea salt		sliced
¼ t	ground pepper	1 c	Granola

Fry onions and garlic in oil until golden, then add meat, and seasonings. Cook for ten minutes over low flame. Add tomatoes and water. Cook for 30 minutes. Add bananas. Cook until meat is tender. Sprinkle Granola on and serve.

Spanish Lamb Chops with Granola

5 garlic cloves	½ t lemon juice
2 T Granola	⅛ t sea salt
1 c vegetable oil, at	14 lamb chops, grilled
room temperature	

In electric blender, blend garlic and Granola together. Very slowly blend in oil, then lemon juice, and salt. Serve lamb chops covered with this sauce.

Granola Moussaka
A delicious adaptation of a delectable and famous Greek dish.

1 lb ground lamb	½ t ground pepper
2 garlic cloves, minced	2 t oregano, ground
1 large onion, sliced	2 t basil, ground
2 T vegetable oil	1 t mint, ground
1 large eggplant, cut	8 oz cream cheese
in ½-inch slices	1 c cream
2 c stewed tomatoes	½ c Cheddar cheese,
1 c tomato sauce	grated
1 t sea salt	1 c Granola

Brown meat, garlic, and onion in 1 Tbsp. oil. Brown eggplant separately in 1 Tbsp. oil. When meat is browned, add tomatoes, tomato sauce, and seasonings. In oiled baking dish, alternate layers of eggplant and meat sauce until all are used. Bake at 325° for 30 minutes. Whip cream cheese and cream, and stir in grated cheese and Granola. Cover moussaka with this sauce and bake another 30 minutes.

Lamb and Ham with Granola

2 lbs	lamb, cut in bite-sized pieces from leg	1	slice ham, diced
2	garlic cloves, minced	1	onion, chopped
2 T	vegetable oil	1 c	tomatoes, sliced
½ t	sea salt	6	red bell peppers, cut in strips
¼ t	ground pepper	¾ c	Granola

Fry lamb and garlic in hot oil. Sprinkle with salt and pepper while frying. When lamb is browned, add ham and onion. Once onion is tender, add tomatoes and peppers. Fry slowly till lamb is tender. Then stir in Granola.

Onion-Lamb Sauté with Granola

4	onions, chopped	½ t	sea salt
3 T	vegetable oil	¼ t	ground pepper
4	garlic cloves, minced	1 t	paprika
2 lbs	lamb, cut in bite-sized pieces from leg	1 T	parsley, chopped
juice of 1 lemon		1 c	Granola

Sauté onions in oil until golden, then add garlic, meat, lemon juice, salt, pepper, and paprika. Fry until meat is tender, adding parsley in the last few minutes. Stir in Granola just before serving.

FISH

Shrimp-Salmon-Granola Celebration

3 T	butter	2	hard-boiled eggs, cut up
½ c	shrimp, cooked and shelled	½ c	Granola
½ c	salmon, cooked and flaked	½	cucumber, peeled and sliced thinly
1 c	rice cooked		

In melted butter in skillet over low heat, stir shrimp,

salmon, and rice. A minute later, add eggs. Continue stirring until mixture is heated. Add Granola and cucumber.

Dill Halibut Granola

2 T butter	½ t ground pepper
2 T vegetable oil	1 T crushed dill seeds
¼ c whole-wheat pastry flour	¼ t paprika
	1 t tamari
2 c milk	¼ c Granola
1½ t sea salt	3 lbs halibut fillets, diced

Melt butter with oil in a saucepan and mix in flour. Slowly add milk, stirring rapidly. Add salt, pepper, paprika, dill, tamari, and Granola. Simmer for ten minutes. Add halibut to the sauce, still simmering. Simmer for four minutes.

Granola-Fried Fish Fillets

¼ c Granola, ground	2 lbs fish fillets
1 t sea salt	½ c vegetable oil

Combine Granola and salt. Dredge fillets in this mixture. Heat oil and add fish. Brown on both sides and serve.

Granola Casserole of Sole and Corn

2 c Granola	juice of 1 lemon
½ c stock	1¼ c milk
3 T vegetable oil	2 eggs, beaten
2 c corn, cooked	½ t sea salt
2 c sole, cooked, boned, and flaked	¼ t ground pepper
	½ t rosemary, crumbled

Combine Granola, stock, and oil. Spread half of mixture in bottom of oiled casserole. Layer on the corn, then the fish. Sprinkle fish with lemon juice. Finish with rest of Granola mixture. Mix remaining ingredients and pour over casserole. Cover and bake for 30 minutes at 350°.

Granola Trout in Sauce

1 c sour cream	2 T parsley, chopped
2 T lemon juice	finely
1 t sea salt	2 lbs trout, cleaned
1 t tamari	1 c mushrooms, sliced
¼ c onion, grated	⅓ c Granola
½ t mustard powder	1 T paprika

Stir together the sour cream, lemon juice, tamari, onion, mustard, and parsley. Place fish and mushrooms in sauce in casserole and dip sauce over fish. Sprinkle Granola and paprika over fish. Bake at 300° for 20 minutes.

Croquettes of Cod in Granola

¾ c cod, boned, skinned, and diced	2 T parsley, chopped
¾ c vegetable oil	1½ c cold milk
6 T whole-wheat flour	1 egg, separated
¼ c onion, chopped	5 T Granola

Cook onion slowly in 2 Tbsp. oil in a saucepan. Once onion is golden, add cod and stir in parsley and 4 Tbsp. of the flour. When mixture is dry, remove from stove and gradually stir in milk. Cook over moderate heat for 25 minutes, stirring with increasing frequency. Remove from fire again and blend in egg yolk. Cool thoroughly. Combine Granola and 2 Tbsp. of the flour. Separately, beat egg white slightly. With hands, form fish mixture into small croquettes, dipping each in the egg white, then the Granola mixture. In a large frypan, heat the remaining oil and fry croquettes, browning them evenly. Remove, drain on paper, cool slightly, and serve.

Salmon Curry with Granola

2 onions, sliced	4 c potatoes, cooked and
1 garlic clove, minced	cubed
1 T curry powder	1 c celery, chopped
1 t cumin, ground	1 apple, grated
2 T butter	½ t sea salt
1 lb salmon, boned and	¼ t ground pepper
coarsely flaked	½ c yogurt
	¾ c Granola

Sauté onion, garlic, curry powder, and cumin in butter in frypan. After a few minutes, add salmon and potatoes, and stir gently over low heat for 20 minutes. Add celery, apple, salt, and pepper, and cook a few more minutes to blend. Stir in yogurt and sprinkle Granola on.

Swordfish with Granola

1½ lbs swordfish	⅛ t ground pepper
3 T butter	¼ t thyme
2 onions, sliced	1 T whole-wheat flour
1 c white wine	¼ c Granola
1 t sea salt	

In large skillet, heat 2 Tbsp. of the butter and cook fish and onions in it, until fish is browned. Stir in wine, salt, pepper, and thyme and bring to boil. Cover, and simmer for 40 minutes. Remove fish to serving dish and keep warm. Combine rest of the butter with flour, add mixture to skillet, and cook briefly until sauce thickens. Stir in Granola and pour over fish.

African Fish

3 onions, sliced	1 small can anchovies
1 T vegetable oil	½ c peanut butter
4 tomatoes, cut in eighths	1 c Granola, ground
	1 T curry powder
½ lb small fish, cleaned and cut up	¼ t sea salt
	2½ c water

Sauté onions in oil until golden, then add tomatoes and cook for five minutes. Add fish and anchovies, peanut butter, Granola, curry powder, salt, and water. Cook uncovered over low flame for 30 minutes.

Granola Fish Patties

½ c Granola, ground	¼ t ground pepper
2 eggs, beaten	1 c fish fillet, chopped
⅓ c milk	1 onion, chopped
½ t sea salt	¼ c vegetable oil

Combine Granola, eggs, milk, salt, and pepper. Add fish and onion. Heat oil, and fry spoonfuls of fish mixture on both sides.

STUFFINGS, SAUCES, AND DUMPLINGS

Each of the stuffing recipes makes enough for one chicken; double the recipe for turkey.

Celery-Granola Stuffing

2 t celery salt	2 c Granola
¼ t ground pepper	2 c celery, chopped
¼ t dill seed	½ c warm milk
1 T whole-wheat flour	⅓ c butter, melted

Mix seasonings and flour together, stir into Granola, then add other ingredients.

Apple-Granola Stuffing

3 apples, grated	¼ c Cheddar cheese,
½ c onion, grated	grated
½ c celery, chopped	1 T honey
1 garlic clove, minced	1 t sea salt
2 eggs, beaten	3 T parsley, minced
2 c Granola	¼ t cloves, ground

Mix together all ingredients. Makes about four cups.

Rice and Granola Stuffing

2 c stock	1¼ c Granola
giblets from chicken	1 t sea salt
(or turkey)	¼ t ground pepper
3 T vegetable oil	3 T parsley, minced
1 c onion, chopped	1 t tarragon, ground
1 c brown rice, uncooked	

Simmer stock and giblets in covered pot until tender. Sauté onion and rice in oil slowly for 10 minutes. Chop giblets and combine with stock, rice, and onions. Cover and cook slowly for 20 minutes. Stir in rest of ingredients. About four cups.

Yam-Granola Stuffing

2 c yams, cooked and	½ c dried apricots,
puréed	chopped
½ lb pork sausage, cooked	1 c stock
1 c celery, chopped	1 t sea salt
1 onion, grated	¼ t ground pepper
2½ c Granola	⅛ t allspice, ground

Combine all ingredients thoroughly. About five cups.

Peanut Butter and Mustard Sauce with Granola
Especially right with ham.

⅓ c light cream	2 T honey
⅓ c peanut butter	¼ t sea salt
⅓ c Granola, ground	⅛ t ground pepper
3 T mustard (prepared)	½ t coriander, ground

Blend all ingredients (except seasonings) over heat, stirring constantly. Then stir seasonings in.

Cranberry-Granola Sauce
A good one with turkey.

4 c cranberries	1½ c honey
1 c orange juice	½ c Granola

Cook cranberries and orange juice in a covered saucepan for eight minutes. Mix in honey and chill. Stir in the Granola.

Curry Sauce Granola

1 T butter	½ c chicken stock
1 T whole-wheat flour	¼ c Granola, ground
½ c cream	1 T curry powder

Blend butter and flour in top of double boiler. Stir in other ingredients and stir while thickening.

Granola Horseradish Sauce
A hit with roast beef.

¼ c fresh horseradish, grated	½ c vinegar
2 t prepared mustard	1 t honey
¼ c Granola, ground	1 t sea salt
	½ t ground pepper

Mix and heat all ingredients in top of double boiler.

Marla's Raisin-Granola Glaze

Created for ham, and excellent elsewhere, too.

1 c brown sugar	1 T vinegar
1 T cornstarch	1 t grated lemon rind
1 c water	1 T butter, melted
¼ t cloves, ground	¾ c raisins
¼ t sea salt	⅔ c Granola

In a saucepan mix sugar, cornstarch, water, cloves, and salt. Cook over low flame, stirring constantly, until sugar is dissolved. Add vinegar, lemon rind, butter, raisins, and Granola. Cook until heated.

Granola Dumplings

½ c Granola, ground	½ c powdered milk
½ c whole-wheat bread crumbs	2 eggs, beaten
2 T whole-wheat flour	2 T milk
2 T wheat germ	2 T vegetable oil
	⅛ t sea salt

Blend all ingredients thoroughly. Roll into walnut-sized balls. Drop into simmering pot of stew, cover, and simmer for five minutes.

Corn Meal and Granola Dumplings

¾ c corn meal	¼ t dill, ground
¾ c whole-wheat flour	1 T onions, chopped
¼ c Granola	2 T sour cream
1 T baking powder	1 egg, beaten
1 t sea salt	¼ c buttermilk

Combine dry ingredients. Beat together the sour cream, egg, and buttermilk. Mix with the dry ingredients. Drop from spoon into simmering stew, cover, and cook for 14 minutes.

CHAPTER 5

VEGETABLE DISHES WITH GRANOLA

The vegetables here vary from such old stand-bys as peas, squash, potatoes, and carrots, to such relatively uncommon treats as grape leaves, okra, and even chestnuts. There are three basic ways the Granola is utilized with these vegetables, whether in casseroles, loaves, or patties, stuffed vegetables, scalloped, or stirred. In one, Granola is sprinkled over the top of the dish, often in combination with cheese, and provides a crust. Others have Granola mixed in after the dish is cooked, adding its unique crunchiness. And in the third method, the Granola (sometimes ground) is mixed into the makings before cooking, melding into the whole.

French Peas with Granola

2 c	shelled peas	1 t	sea salt
6	lettuce leaves	½ t	ground pepper
2	onions, chopped	3 T	butter
1½ t	honey	½ c	water
1 T	parsley, ground	½ c	Granola

Mix peas, lettuce, onions, honey, parsley, salt, pepper, and 2 Tbsp. butter in a saucepan; let stand for one hour. Then add water, cover, and bring to boil. Cook briskly for 25 minutes, when liquid should be nearly gone. Remove pan from burner and add remaining butter. When butter is melted, stir in Granola.

74

Zucchini-Granola Patties

2	eggs	4	zucchini, chilled and
1 t	sea salt		chopped fine
¼ t	ground pepper	4	green onions,
¼ c	Granola, ground		chopped
⅛ t	cayenne, ground		

Stir eggs, salt, pepper, Granola, and cayenne together. Add zucchini and green onions. Drop batter from tablespoon onto oiled frypan. Brown on both sides, then cover pan and sauté six minutes.

Granola-Stuffed Yellow Squash

2 c	onion, minced	1 t	basil, ground
1	garlic clove, minced	½ t	savory, ground
½ t	sea salt	1 c	Granola
1 T	butter	1	egg, beaten
8	crookneck squash	2 T	Parmesan cheese,
2 T	parsley, chopped		grated

Sauté onion, garlic, and salt in butter until onion is clear. Trim squash, cut in half lengthwise, and spoon out centers. Add squash centers (chopped) and seasonings to frypan and cook until tender. Combine Granola, eggs, and cheese and mix in with squash centers. Steam squash halves until tender and set in oiled casserole or baking pan. Fill squash with the filling. Bake for 30 minutes at 375°.

Granola Baked Squash

3	butternut or acorn	¼ t	sea salt
	squash, halved	⅛ t	mace, ground
3 T	honey	½ c	Granola
3 T	vegetable oil		

Remove seeds and membranes from squash. Arrange squash on baking pan filled ¼-inch high with water. Mix rest of ingredients together, and spoon into cavities of squash halves. Cover and bake at 350° for one hour, uncovering during the final 15 minutes.

Chinese Crunchy Broccoli

2 lbs broccoli, chopped
½ c butter
1 can water chestnuts,
        diced
2 T onion, minced
1 t sea salt
¼ t ground pepper
½ c lemon juice
2 T tamari
¼ c walnuts, chopped
½ c Granola

Cook broccoli in covered saucepan with small amount of boiling salted water for 15 minutes. Drain. Melt butter in same saucepan; add water chestnuts, onion, salt, and pepper. Sauté several minutes. Add lemon juice, tamari, walnuts, and Granola.

Scalloped Corn Granola

2 c corn, cut from cobs
      and chilled
⅓ c milk, simmering
½ t sea salt
⅛ t ground pepper
¾ c Fontina or Cheddar
      cheese, grated
⅓ c Granola

Add corn to milk in saucepan. Heat to simmering, cover, lower heat, and simmer two minutes. Stir in seasonings. Place in oiled casserole. Cover with cheese, then Granola. Broil until cheese melts.

Corn Dinner Pudding

2½ c milk
¼ c Granola, ground
1 t sea salt
1 T vegetable oil
2 c corn, cooked
2 eggs, beaten
1 T green pepper,
      chopped
1 t savory, ground

Combine ½ cup of the milk with Granola and salt. Heat 2 cups milk in top of double boiler. Gradually add Granola mixture to hot milk and blend well. Cover and cook, stirring frequently until mixture thickens. Remove from heat and stir in the remaining ingredients. Put in oiled casserole and set in shallow pan of hot water. Bake at 350° for 30 minutes, until center is firm.

Tomatoes, Green Onions, and Granola

4	tomatoes, peeled and diced	½ t	basil, ground
8	green onions, chopped	½ t	sea salt
		¼ t	ground pepper
1 t	molasses	¼ c	Granola
		½ c	Swiss cheese, grated

Put tomatoes into an oiled casserole that can be used on top of stove. Cook over burner for five minutes. Add green onions, molasses, basil, salt, and pepper. Simmer eight minutes, partially covered so juice can evaporate. Remove from burner and sprinkle with Granola and cheese.

Granola Eggplant Parmesan

1	large eggplant, cut into ½-inch slices	2	garlic cloves, crushed
2 T	vegetable oil	2 T	onion, grated
3	tomatoes, diced	2 T	green pepper, grated
½ t	sea salt	2 T	carrot, grated
¼ t	ground pepper	½ c	Parmesan cheese, grated
1 T	parsley, chopped		
¼ t	oregano, ground	1 c	Granola
¼ t	thyme, ground	½ lb	Mozzarella cheese, sliced
¼ t	rosemary, crumbled		

Sauté the eggplant in oil until slightly browned; drain on paper towels. In a saucepan, mix tomatoes, seasonings, and grated vegetables, cover, and simmer 15 minutes. Then blend in Parmesan cheese and Granola. In an oiled casserole, place a layer of eggplant, cover with half the tomato mixture, then half the Mozzarella cheese, and repeat layers. Bake at 350° for 30 minutes.

Granola-Stuffed Green Peppers

8	green peppers	1 c	Granola
1 lb	hamburger	1	egg, beaten
1 t	sea salt	½ c	evaporated milk
¼ t	ground pepper	2 c	tomato sauce
¼ t	thyme, ground	1 t	basil, ground
1 T	parsley, chopped	1 T	Parmesan cheese,
¼ c	black olives, pitted		grated
	and chopped fine	½ c	water
1	onion, minced		

Slice off and discard the stem end of each pepper; spoon out and discard the seeds. Add the salt, pepper, thyme, and parsley to the hamburger, then stir in the olives, onion, Granola, egg, and milk. Pack this mixture into the peppers. Place the peppers in a deep casserole. Stir together the tomato sauce, basil, cheese, and water, then pour over the peppers. Bake in a 400° oven for one hour.

Cheese, Spinach, and Granola

2 lbs	spinach, washed,	1 T	honey
	dried and shredded	2 t	whole-wheat flour
3 T	butter	⅓ c	cream
½ t	sea salt	⅓ c	milk
¼ t	ground pepper	3 T	Swiss cheese, grated
⅛ t	nutmeg, grated	¾ c	Granola

Melt 1 Tbsp. butter in a frypan, add spinach, and cook for five minutes, stirring often. Sprinkle on salt, pepper, nutmeg, honey, and 1 tsp. of the flour, and mix well. Cook for two minutes, stirring. Remove pan from burner. Stir in the cream, return pan to fire, and bring to boil, stirring; then lower the flame, cover, and simmer for 20 minutes. Remove from fire. Add 1 Tbsp. of butter and blend in. In another

frypan, melt 1 Tbsp. butter, stir in 1 tsp. flour, add milk
and cook, stirring, until it boils. Lower flame, add 2 Tbsp.
cheese and cook, stirring constantly, for five minutes, until
smooth. In bottom of casserole, spread 3 Tbsp. of this sauce,
add spinach, and cover with remaining sauce. Sprinkle with
Granola, then remaining cheese. Bake at 500° for 3 minutes.

Cabbage in Apples and Granola

2	apples, cored and quartered	1 t	caraway seeds
½ c	honey	1½ t	sea salt
½ c	vinegar	⅛ t	ground pepper
2 T	vegetable oil	1	head cabbage, chopped
½ c	water	½ c	Granola

Blend apples, honey, vinegar, oil, water, seeds, salt, and
pepper in electric blender. Pour over cabbage in saucepan
and simmer for one hour. Mix in Granola and serve.

Granola-Cauliflower Bake

3 c	cauliflower, cooked and chopped	¼ c	vegetable oil
½ c	stock, seasoned	½ c	cheese, grated
		1 c	Granola

In electric blender, blend cauliflower in stock. Pour into
oiled casserole. Stir in other ingredients. Bake at 350° for 20
minutes.

Mushrooms with Granola

1	onion, diced	½ t	sea salt
1	clove garlic, minced	⅛ t	ground pepper
3 T	butter	¼ t	nutmeg
1 lb	mushrooms, sliced	1½ c	Granola

Sauté onions and garlic in butter, add mushrooms, and
cook for ten minutes. Add seasonings and Granola.

Granola Asparagus in Cream

1 lb asparagus, cut in 1-inch lengths	¼ c heavy cream
1 c milk	2 t honey
½ c mayonnaise	½ c Granola

In saucepan, cook asparagus in milk for 15 minutes, until tender. Cool. Whip mayonnaise, cream, and honey together, stir in Granola, and stir this sauce into the asparagus.

Beets Granola

1 onion, sliced	3 T vinegar
2 T butter	½ c honey
¼ t cloves, ground	2½ c beets, cooked and
¼ t dill, ground	sliced
½ t sea salt	½ c Granola

Blend all ingredients in electric blender (except beets and Granola) until smooth. Pour over beets in saucepan. Sprinkle Granola on top. Simmer for ten minutes, stirring often.

Carrot-Granola Casserole

3 c carrots, cooked	½ t tarragon, ground
4 eggs	2 T honey
1 onion, diced	1 T vegetable oil
½ t sea salt	½ c Granola
3 T parsley, chopped	

In electric blender, blend all ingredients (except Granola). Pour into bowl and stir in Granola. Pour into oiled casserole and set casserole in a shallow pan of water. Bake for 30 minutes at 350°.

Carrot-Stir with Granola

2 c carrots, shredded	2 T tamari
2 eggs, beaten	1 c Swiss cheese, grated
½ onion, minced	1 c Granola
1 t tarragon, ground	1 c brown rice, cooked
1 c stock, seasoned	

Mix all ingredients together in a skillet over low heat. Cover and cook for a half-hour, stirring occasionally.

Granola Okra Fries

½ c Granola, ground	1 T parsley, chopped
½ t sea salt	2 c okra, chilled and
⅛ t ground pepper	sliced
¼ t paprika	¼ c vegetable oil

Mix Granola and seasonings. Toss with okra on waxed paper. Fry in oil until golden.

Sweet Potatoes Granola

1 lb sweet potatoes,	1 t grated lemon peel
cooked and sliced	¼ c Granola
1 T molasses	2 t cinnamon
1 c pineapple slices	

Lay the sweet potatoes in an oiled casserole. Pour molasses over them. Add a layer of pineapple. Sprinkle with Granola, lemon peel, and cinnamon. Heat at 350° for 10 minutes.

Marla's Granola Scalloped Potatoes

5 medium-sized	½ c Granola
potatoes	1½ c milk
1½ T whole-wheat flour	2 T butter, melted
½ t sea salt	½ c Cheddar cheese,
½ t ground pepper	grated
1 T parsley, ground	

Pare and slice potatoes ¼ inch thick. Oil a casserole dish. Cover with a layer of potatoes. Sprinkle with flour, salt, pepper, parsley, and Granola. Repeat until all potatoes are used up. Pour milk and melted butter over potatoes. Top with grated cheese. Cover. Bake in a 375° oven for 20 minutes. Remove cover and cook for one-half hour longer or until potatoes are tender.

Granola-Stuffed Potatoes

2 potatoes, equal in size	1 T onion, minced
	1 t parsley, chopped
1½ T butter	1 T Granola, ground

Bake potatoes. Slice in half lengthwise and spoon out most of their insides. Mix insides with butter, onion, parsley, and Granola. Fill skins again and brown in oven.

Granola-Potato Loaf

1 onion, chopped	½ c soy grits
2 garlic cloves, minced	½ c stock
1 T butter	1 egg, beaten
1 c Granola, ground	1 t sea salt
3 c potatoes, cooked and puréed	¼ t ground pepper
	¼ t nutmeg, ground
1 c celery, chopped	3 T parsley, minced

Sauté onion and garlic in butter, then combine all ingredients. Turn into oiled loaf pan. Bake at 350° for 40 minutes.

Potato-Blender Casserole with Granola

6 potatoes, quartered	½ t sea salt
1 onion, quartered	⅛ t ground pepper
1 c Granola	¼ t thyme, ground
2 eggs	½ c walnuts
3 T vegetable oil	

Blend and mix all ingredients (except walnuts) in electric blender. Turn into oiled casserole and sprinkle walnuts on top. Bake at 350° for 45 minutes.

Granola Beans and Tomatoes

1	onion, chopped	2 lbs	tomatoes, chopped
1 T	vegetable oil	1 t	curry powder
1 lb	green beans, stringed and broken	1 t	sea salt
		1 c	Granola, ground

Sauté onions in oil until golden. Add beans and cook, stirring regularly, for ten minutes. Add tomatoes and cook for five minutes. Stir in curry powder, salt, and Granola. Cook for ten minutes more.

Vegetable Granola Loaf

1 c	carrots, grated	⅓ c	tomato juice
1 c	beets, grated	2	eggs, beaten
1	onion, grated	½ t	sea salt
1	green pepper, minced	¼ t	ground pepper
1 c	soybeans, cooked	1 t	oregano, ground
½ c	Granola	1 t	parsley, ground

Stir together all ingredients and turn into oiled loaf pan. Bake at 350° for an hour.

Vegetable Chow Mein with Granola

2 T	vegetable oil	½ c	tofu, diced
1 c	celery, thinly sliced	¼ c	parsley, chopped
1 c	green pepper, thinly sliced	2 T	tamari
		1⅛ c	water
1 c	onion, thinly sliced	1 T	arrowroot, ground
1 c	bean sprouts	1 c	Granola
½ c	mushrooms, sliced		

In frypan, heat oil over medium burner, then add all vegetables, tofu, and parsley. Stir in tamari and ⅛ cup of the water, then cover and simmer 15 minutes. Add 1 cup water and arrowroot and stir until sauce is thickened. Stir in Granola.

Granola in Grape Leaves

1 lb onions, chopped	1½ t sea salt
2 garlic cloves, minced	⅛ t ground pepper
¾ c vegetable oil	1⅓ c Granola
2 c brown rice, uncooked	60 grape leaves, salted
4 c water	1 cucumber, peeled
½ t thyme, ground	2 c tomato sauce
¼ t mint, ground	

Sauté onions and garlic in oil until golden, then add rice and continue cooking until rice is slightly browned. Add water, thyme, mint, salt, and pepper, bring to boil, then lower heat and simmer, covered, for 50 minutes. Off heat, stir in Granola, and let cool. Fill each grape leaf with 1 Tbsp. of the mixture and fold. Set close together in baking pan. Put cucumber in electric blender, then add to tomato sauce. Pour sauce over filled grape leaves, and cover. Bake at 350° for 40 minutes.

Chestnut Loaf

1 lb chestnuts, without shells	1 c walnuts
	6 eggs, beaten
¼ lb mushrooms, chopped	¾ c milk
½ lb ground lamb, cooked	½ c parsley, chopped
	1 t sea salt
1 onion, minced	¼ t ground pepper
1 c celery, chopped	¼ t sage, ground
2 c Granola	¼ t thyme, ground

Combine all ingredients and put in oiled casserole or loaf pan. Bake at 400° for one hour.

Chestnut–Sour Cream Casserole with Granola

1 lb chestnuts, shelled and chopped	1 T parsley, minced
2 onions, chopped	2 T basil, minced
1 bell pepper, chopped	¾ c Parmesan cheese, grated
1 c milk	¾ c Granola
½ t sea salt	1 c sour cream
¼ t ground pepper	

Mix chestnuts, onion, and bell pepper, and place in oiled casserole. Combine milk and seasonings and pour over. Cover with cheese and Granola. Bake at 375° for 45 minutes, then stir in sour cream.

Sweet-and-Sour Granola Chestnuts

Very special as a side dish, or as a treat.

4 c water	1 t cloves, ground
2 c honey	1 T cinnamon, ground
2 lemons, with rind slivered	1 t ginger, ground
1 orange, with rind slivered	1 lb chestnuts
	1 c Granola

In saucepan, bring water and honey to a boil and add rinds of lemons and orange; lower heat. Thinly slice one of the lemons and the orange and add to the simmering liquid. Juice the other lemon into the saucepan. Add seasonings and chestnuts. Simmer for one hour, stirring occasionally. Stir in Granola and cool.

Curried Soybeans with Granola

1 onion, chopped finely	¼ c Granola
1 apple, chopped finely	½ t ginger, ground
1 T curry powder	½ t paprika, ground
2 T vegetable oil	1 T tamari
⅓ c soybeans, cooked	1 c yogurt

Sauté the onion, apple, and curry powder in oil until onion is transparent. Stir in soybeans and Granola, then ginger, paprika, and tamari. Remove to a serving dish and stir in yogurt.

Granola and Beans in Sour Cream

1 onion, sliced	½ c sour cream
1 T butter	1 T honey
½ c Granola	¼ t sea salt
2 T soybeans, cooked	⅛ t ground pepper
½ c kidney beans, cooked	½ t ginger, ground
½ c butter beans, cooked	

Sauté onion in butter till golden. Stir in the Granola and beans, then the sour cream and honey, then the seasonings. Let blend over heat for five minutes.

Vegetable Croquettes

2 c kidney beans, cooked and puréed	½ c stock
	1 t sea salt
1 c split peas, cooked and puréed	¼ t ground pepper
	1 t chervil, ground
1 c lentils, cooked and puréed	1 egg
	2 T milk
¼ c soy grits	1 c Granola, ground

Combine beans, peas, lentils, grits, salt, pepper, chervil, and stock. Shape into balls and flatten slightly. Beat eggs and milk together. Dip croquettes in egg mixture and roll in Granola. Broil until brown on all sides.

Granola-Soybean-Barley Casserole

1½ c	Granola	1	carrot, grated
1½ c	soybeans, cooked	1 c	stewed tomatoes
½ c	whole barley, hulled and soaked	1 t	sea salt
		¼ t	ground pepper
2	celery stalks, diced	½ t	savory, ground
2	onions, sliced	½ t	chervil, ground
1	boiled potato, diced	1 t	dill seeds

Mix together all ingredients and turn into an oiled casserole. Bake at 350° for 30 minutes.

Granola-Seed Loaf with Lentils

1 c	dried lentils, cooked	2	eggs, beaten
½ c	grated beets	1 T	vinegar
1	onion, diced	2 t	lemon juice
½ c	celery, diced	½ c	parsley, chopped
¾ c	sunflower seeds	1 t	sea salt
¾ c	sesame seeds	¼ t	ground pepper
1¼ c	Granola	1 t	sage, ground

Mix all ingredients together well. Turn into oiled casserole. Bake 40 minutes at 325°.

Granola Casserole

1	onion, sliced	½ t	sea salt
¼ c	mushrooms, sliced	⅛ t	ground pepper
3 T	vegetable oil	3 T	parsley, minced
3	eggs, beaten	1 T	basil, ground
1½ c	Granola	¼ t	sage, ground
1 c	walnuts	2 T	honey
½ c	powdered milk	½ to 1 c	water

Sauté onion and mushrooms in oil. Mix with remaining ingredients, adding enough water to moisten. Bake at 325° for 45 minutes.

CHAPTER 6

GRANOLA WITH EGGS AND CHEESE

This is primarily an egg chapter, with cheese a regular and important companion. The two are, of course, highly complimentary, and Granola makes for a happy trio, adding its beneficially contrasting texture and taste.

Once we look beyond the familiar egg approaches—scrambled, creamed, baked, and deviled—we discover that eggs are fancy things, especially when melded with cheese. The names themselves suggest rich cultures and satisfied palates—timbales, soufflé, fondue, Benedict, quiche, Welsh rarebit.

And there's an egg nog—a healthy one.

Granola Scrambled Eggs

4	bacon strips	½ t	sea salt
¼ c	Granola	⅛ t	ground pepper
4	eggs	1 T	butter
¼ c	milk		

Cook the bacon in a frypan, remove, and pour off excess fat. Pour in Granola and allow to brown slightly while picking up the bacon flavor. Crumble bacon and stir into Granola. Mix eggs, milk, salt, and pepper thoroughly and pour over Granola. As the mixture thickens, lift from the bottom and sides, so the uncooked part flows to the bottom. Cook to desirable doneness.

Chinese Scrambled Eggs with Granola

It's surprising how oriental Granola can become in the right context. Sweet-and-sour Granola might be your choice here.

1 lb	sausage (bulk or link), in small pieces	6	eggs, beaten
⅓ c	celery, chopped	⅓ c	milk
⅓ c	green onions, chopped	½ c	Granola
½ c	bean sprouts	½ t	sea salt
		⅛ t	ground pepper

Brown sausage lightly in skillet and pour off excess fat. Add celery and onions; cook for three minutes. Add bean sprouts. Combine eggs, milk, Granola, salt, and pepper, and pour over sausage and vegetables. Cook over low heat about ten minutes, stirring occasionally, until eggs are set and vegetables remain crispy.

Granola and Cheese Soufflé

½ c	Granola	1 c	Cheddar cheese, grated
4	egg yolks, well beaten	4	egg whites, stiffly beaten
1 t	mustard powder		
¼ t	ground pepper		

Stir together Granola, egg yolks, mustard, and pepper. Gradually add cheese to mixture, stirring constantly. Fold in stiff egg whites. Pour into oiled one-quart casserole set in a pan of hot water. Bake at 375° for about 30 minutes, or until set.

Granola Omelet

4	eggs, at room temperature for one hour	1 T	cream or milk
2 T	Granola, ground	½ t	sea salt
		2 T	butter

Mix all ingredients except butter, beating lightly until blended. Heat butter in frying pan until bubbling and very slightly brown. Add egg mixture. After about 30 seconds, lift one edge of the omelet so that the uncooked egg can slide beneath and be cooked, and continue this process all around the pan until no liquid egg remains. Take pan off flame, fold one-third of the omelet over onto the rest of the omelet, and fold the remaining one-third over the first. Turn the omelet onto a plate and serve at once.

Creamed Eggs Granola

1 T butter	¼ c peas, cooked
1 T whole-wheat flour	¼ c Swiss cheese, grated
1¼ c milk	4 to 6 hard-cooked eggs,
1 garlic clove, minced	shelled and diced
½ t sea salt	whole-wheat toast
¼ c Granola	paprika

Melt butter in saucepan and stir flour in. Add milk and stir constantly until it boils; then lower heat. Add garlic, salt, Granola, and peas. Stir cheese in and cook, stirring constantly, for five minutes. Stir eggs into the sauce. As soon as eggs have heated through, serve over the toast and sprinkle with paprika.

Nori Egg

1 T butter	1 t sea salt
1¼ c Granola (approx.)	¼ t ground pepper
4 to 6 eggs, beaten	1 garlic clove, minced

Melt butter in a casserole that can be used on a burner. Off the flame, cover the bottom of the casserole with Granola and stir it to coat with butter. Combine eggs with salt, pepper, and garlic, and pour into casserole. Sprinkle more Granola on top. Bake at 350°.

Granola Egg Fondue

½ c butter	2 to 2¼ c milk
3 T whole-wheat flour	5 egg yolks, slightly
½ t sea salt	beaten
½ t ground pepper	¼ c Granola
2 garlic cloves,	¾ c Parmesan cheese,
minced	grated

French bread, celery, carrot, green pepper, and apple in bite-sized pieces

Melt butter in saucepan, add flour, and stir until frothy. Add salt, pepper, garlic, and 2 cups milk. Cook, stirring constantly, until thick. Pour small amount of sauce into egg yolks, stirring constantly. Pour this egg mixture into rest of sauce and stir about two minutes until thickened. Stir in Granola, then cheese. The sauce should be thick enough to coat the food pieces without dripping.

Eggs Benedict

16 slices of Canadian	1 green onion, diced
bacon, broiled	2 T lemon juice
4 whole-wheat English	½ t sea salt
muffins—split,	⅛ t cayenne
toasted, and buttered	1 garlic clove, diced
8 poached eggs	½ c hot water
2 eggs	¼ c Granola
½ c butter	1 T parsley, minced

Put 2 slices of bacon on each muffin half, then cover with a poached egg. Blend together in electric blender the 2 eggs, butter, green onion, lemon juice, salt, cayenne, and garlic. With motor still on, slowly add hot water. Blend until smooth. Pour into top of double boiler and cook over hot water, stirring constantly, until thick. Cover each muffin with this sauce and garnish with Granola and parsley.

Granola Quiche Lorraine

Granola pie shell pastry (see page 158).

8 bacon slices, diced	1 c Swiss cheese, grated
½ c green onions, chopped	½ c Granola
6 eggs, beaten	2 c light cream
1 t sea salt	

Line pastry into 9-inch pan. Fry bacon, adding onions part way through, and drain off excess fat. Cool slightly. Stir together eggs, cheese, Granola, salt, and bacon mixture. Add cream, blend well, and pour into pie shell. Bake at 375° for about 35 minutes, or until golden brown and set.

Granola Timbales

1½ T butter	½ c Granola
1 T whole-wheat flour	1½ t chopped pimiento
½ t sea salt	1½ t tamari
⅛ t ground pepper	1 t dry mustard
1½ c milk	3 eggs, beaten
1½ c Cheddar or other	
sharp cheese, chopped	

Melt butter in frypan and blend in flour, salt, and pepper. Pour milk in and cook over low heat, stirring constantly, until thick. Add cheese, Granola, pimiento, tamari, and mustard, and stir until cheese is melted; remove from heat. Add cheese mixture to eggs, stirring constantly. Pour into four or five oiled custard cups. Set cups in shallow baking pan and pour boiling water around them to a depth of one inch. Bake in a 325° oven for 45 minutes or until firm. To serve, remove from cups.

Granola-Stuffed Eggs

3 eggs, hard-cooked, shelled, and halved lengthwise	2 T Granola, ground
	⅛ t sea salt
	⅛ t ground pepper
2 T mayonnaise	⅛ t paprika, ground

Remove yolks from whites of eggs. Crumble yolks with fork and combine with mayonnaise, Granola, salt, pepper, and paprika. Fill egg halves with the yolk mixture and chill.

Curried Eggs Granola
Use the Curried Granola if you desire an extra punch.

2 T butter	⅛ t sea salt
1 small onion, chopped	⅛ t ground pepper
2 t curry powder	8 hard-boiled eggs, shelled and quartered
1 c chicken stock	
¼ c Granola, ground	

Heat butter in a skillet and cook the onion until golden. Stir in the curry powder, then add the stock, Granola, salt, and pepper, continuing to stir now and then. When sauce is thick, add the eggs and stir them gently for a few minutes.

Egg Patties with Granola

4 zucchini, grated	¼ c cheese, grated
1 onion, grated	1 t sea salt
½ c Granola, ground	¼ t ground pepper
3 eggs, beaten	

Blend ingredients together and drop by spoonfuls onto a heated griddle. Brown on both sides.

Spanish Eggs in a Nest

6 small, soft rolls	3 T butter
6 T milk	6 egg yolks

¼ t   sea salt   2 T Granola
5   egg whites   ½ c vegetable oil

Slice the tops from the rolls (the tops will not be used).
Remove the soft interior, being careful not to pierce the
sides. Pour 1 Tbsp. milk into each roll, then put ½ Tbsp.
butter and an egg yolk in each. Sprinkle salt on the yolks.
Beat the egg whites till they peak stiffly, pile them equally
on the yolks, and sprinkle with Granola. Heat the oil hot
and fry the rolls in it, spooning oil onto the whites until they
puff and brown lightly.

Granola Welsh Rarebit

1 T butter   1t tamari
4 c grated cheese   2   egg yolks, beaten
1 c beer   slightly
¼ t dry mustard   ½ c Granola
¼ t paprika   buttered whole-wheat
1 t sea salt   toast

In the top of a double boiler, melt the butter and cheese
over water at a simmer. Stirring steadily, add the beer and
seasonings. Beat 2 Tbsp. of the cheese mixture into the yolks,
then stir this into the double boiler again. Add the Granola
and continue stirring for a minute. Pour over pieces of toast
and serve.

Healthy Eggnog

1   egg   ⅛ c Granola, ground
¼ c powdered milk   ½ t vanilla extract
1 T date sugar   ⅛ t nutmeg, ground
⅔ c milk   ⅛ t cinnamon, ground

Blend egg, powdered milk, sugar, and half the milk. Add
remaining milk, Granola, and vanilla, and beat until foamy.
Top with nutmeg and cinnamon.

CHAPTER 7

GRAIN AND PASTA DISHES WITH GRANOLA

Granola itself is a concoction of grains, of course, so it is among family here. The danger in this is that the Granola will disappear—absorb moisture, become puffy and ambiguous, and fade into the background. So it often is added at the last moment, to let it retain its crispness. The pleasure in this family reunion is that "mod" Granola adds something that is beyond the experience of its old-world cousins.

Brown rice, the other grains, and pasta and dishes made with them (pilaf, risotto, polenta, lasagna) do have an old-world, perhaps peasant, quality that serves as a valuable reminder of civilizations more in touch with nature.

BROWN RICE

Granola Risotto

1	cabbage, grated	⅓ c	Granola
4 c	vegetable stock	1 t	sea salt
2 c	brown rice, uncooked	¼ t	ground pepper
¼ c	tomato paste		

Simmer cabbage in the stock six minutes, then add rice and cook, covered, for 40 minutes. Stir in tomato paste, Granola, salt, and pepper, and serve.

Curried Rice Granola

2 T butter	1¼ c brown rice, uncooked
1 onion, sliced	¼ c soy grits
1 apple, cored and sliced	½ c yogurt
1 T curry powder	½ c Granola
3 c stock	

Melt butter in skillet and add onion, apple, and curry powder. Bring stock to boil in saucepan and add rice, soy grits, and curry mixture. Cover and reduce heat; simmer for one hour. Stir in yogurt and Granola.

Indian Rice with Granola

¼ t saffron, ground	2 c brown rice, cooked
1 t cumin, ground	and hot
½ c water	¼ c Granola
2 T butter	

Add saffron and cumin to water and let sit five minutes. Stir butter into rice. Pour saffron water over rice. Add Granola and mix well.

Creamy Avocados Granola

2 c Granola	3 avocados, peeled,
1 c brown rice, cooked	halved, and pitted
1 c thick cream	2 c Swiss cheese, grated
	1 c sour cream

Mix Granola, rice, and cream. Form this onto avocado halves. Place close together in baking dish. Blend cheese and sour cream and pour some over each half. Bake at 350° until sauce starts bubbling.

Nutful Rice Loaf

1 qt milk
3 c Granola
4   eggs, beaten
3 c brown rice, cooked
1   onion, chopped

2 T vegetable oil
1 t sea salt
3 T sage, ground
2 c walnuts, chopped

Pour 2 cups milk into Granola and let sit for five minutes. Stir together eggs and rice and add to the Granola mixture. Sauté onion in oil and add to mixture. Mix in all remaining ingredients. Form into large loaf pan or casserole and place this in a pan of hot water in oven. Bake for one hour at 350°.

Cheerful Rice

1   onion, chopped
¼ c dried apricots, chopped
¼ c raisins
¼ c dried apples, chopped
⅓ c sesame seeds

2 T vegetable oil
¼ c butter
½ t cloves, ground
½ t sea salt
¾ c Granola
1 c brown rice, cooked

Sauté onion, dried fruits, and sesame seeds in oil until onion is golden. Stir in the butter, cloves, and salt, and then mix with the Granola and rice. Turn into oiled casserole and bake for 20 minutes at 350°.

Rice and Granola Pudding

3 c milk
½ c water
½ c brown rice, uncooked
1 T rice polish

½ c honey
1 T cinnamon, ground
1 c Granola

Combine the milk and water in a saucepan, bring to a boil, add the rice, cover, and simmer for 20 minutes. Take about ¼ cup of the liquid from the pan and blend in the rice polish to make a paste. Add this to the rice and simmer

20 additional minutes. Stir in the honey and cinnamon. Pour into serving bowl, cover with Granola and press in; chill.

OTHER GRAINS

Wild Rice Granola Loaf

4 c water	1 c celery, chopped
1½ t sea salt	2 T vegetable oil
½ c wild rice	¼ c parsley, chopped
½ c brown rice	2 t cumin, ground
½ c buckwheat	2 T butter
2 onions, chopped	½ c Granola

Bring water and salt to a boil; add wild rice, brown rice, and buckwheat. Cover, reduce heat, and simmer 40 minutes to one hour. In a skillet, sauté onions and celery in oil; add onion mixture, parsley, cumin, butter, and Granola to the cooked grains. Spoon into oiled casserole dish and bake at 350° for 30 minutes.

Mixed Grains

¼ c whole grain wheat	1 t sea salt
¼ c whole grain rye	¼ t ground pepper
2 c water	¼ t saffron, ground
1 onion, chopped	½ t cumin, ground
1 green pepper, chopped	½ c brown rice, uncooked
2 garlic cloves, minced	3 tomatoes, quartered
2 T butter	¼ c Granola

Soak the wheat grains and rye grains in the water overnight. Sauté onion, green pepper, and garlic in butter until golden. Drain water from the wheat and rye grains into a saucepan, add enough water to make 2 cups, add seasonings, and bring to a boil. Add all three grains, sautéed vegetables, and tomatoes, and cover. Lower heat and simmer for one hour. Stir in Granola and serve.

Crunchy Pilaf

Granola adds zest to pilaf (bulgar wheat). If there is plenty of powdered milk in the Granola used here, the protein value of the dish will be higher.

2 c water	1 c pilaf
1 t sea salt	1 c Granola

Heat the water and salt to boiling. Add the pilaf, cover, and reduce the heat to low. Cook for 15 minutes, or until no water is left. Mix in the Granola and serve.

Peasant Pilaf with Granola

2 onions, chopped	1 t parsley, chopped
¼ c vegetable oil	1 t sage, ground
2 c pilaf	½ t allspice, ground
4 c vegetable stock	1 t sea salt
2 tomatoes, sliced	¾ c Granola

Sauté onions in oil until golden, adding pilaf when onion is half done. Bring stock to boil and add pilaf and onions, tomatoes, and seasonings. Reduce heat and simmer 15 minutes. Stir in Granola.

Polenta with Granola and Sausages

2 c corn meal	1 c tomato sauce
2 t sea salt	1 t fennel seeds, ground
1 c cold water	1½ c Granola
4 c boiling water	½ c Parmesan cheese,
¼ c butter	grated
8 pork sausages, cooked	

Mix the corn meal with the salt and cold water in the top of a double boiler over simmering water, and stir in the boiling water. Cover and cook for 30 minutes, stirring occasionally. Then mix in the butter. Cut the sausages into 1-inch lengths and combine with tomato sauce and fennel. Oil a casserole and spread the bottom with half the Granola, then half the hot mush over it, then all the sauce, followed by the rest of the mush, and the rest of the Granola. Sprinkle with cheese. Heat for 15 minutes in a 400° oven.

PASTA

Granola Vegetable Spaghetti

1	onion, diced	2 T	parsley, chopped
3	garlic cloves, minced	1 T	basil, ground
3	zucchini, sliced or diced	1 t	oregano, ground
2	summer squash, sliced	1 t	thyme, ground
1	bunch broccoli, chopped	1 T	cumin, ground
		1 t	cinnamon, ground
2	tomatoes, diced	1 T plus 1 t	sea salt
⅓ lb	whole-wheat or wheat-soy spaghetti	¼ t	ground pepper
		¼ c	butter
2 c	tomato sauce	1 c	Parmesan cheese, grated
3 T	tamari	1 c	Granola

Steam vegetables 15 minutes in covered, oiled frypan. When vegetables have 5 minutes to go, break spaghetti into thirds and drop with 1 Tbsp. salt into boiling water; boil eight minutes. When vegetables are cooked stir in tomato sauce and spices and cover. Once spaghetti is done, drain and mix in with vegetables, leaving uncovered now. Stir in butter and cheese. Sprinkle Granola over top; serve at once.

Crunchy Spaghetti Sauce

⅔ c	boiling water	2	garlic cloves, minced
¼ c	vegetable oil	1	green onion, chopped
2 T	parsley, chopped	¼ c	butter
2 T	basil, ground	8 oz	cream cheese
1 t	thyme, ground	⅓ c	Parmesan cheese, grated
1 t	sea salt		
¼ t	ground pepper	¼ c	Granola

Blend all ingredients (except Granola) in blender for one minute. Add to cooked spaghetti, and stir in Granola.

Granola Lasagna

2½ c water
  1 t sea salt
 12 lasagna strips
1½ c milk

⅔ c powdered milk
1 c Cheddar cheese, grated
½ c Granola
2 T basil, ground

Put water and salt in baking pan and bring to boil over burner. Add lasagna and cover. Lower heat to simmer for ten minutes. Remove lasagna and dry on towels. Add milk and powdered milk to the water and mix. Into milk, alternate layers of lasagna and cheese. Sprinkle top with Granola and basil. Bake at 300° for 15 minutes.

Macaroni, Beans, and Granola

2 c water
1 t sea salt
2 c macaroni shells
2 T butter
2 c cooked, hot pinto beans

4 green onions, chopped
½ c Granola
¼ t ground pepper
1 T parsley, ground

In casserole that can be used on top of stove, bring water and salt to boil, then add macaroni slowly. Cover casserole and lower heat; simmer for ten minutes. Drain macaroni. Add butter, beans, onion, Granola, and seasonings.

Noodles with Pork and Granola Sauce

2	garlic cloves, minced	⅓ c	Granola, ground
2	onions, chopped	¾ lb	whole-wheat
2 T	vegetable oil		noodles
½ lb	salt pork, diced	½ t	ground pepper
3	tomatoes, chopped	½ t	sea salt
6 c	beef bouillon	1 T	parsley, ground
12	slices pork sausage, cooked		

In casserole that can be used on top of stove, sauté garlic and onion in oil with salt pork. Once onion is golden, add tomatoes. Fry until sauce thickens. Add beef bouillon and sausage and boil five minutes. Then blend a little liquid from the casserole into the Granola and pour this paste into the casserole. Mix well, add noodles and seasonings, and boil slowly for 20 minutes, stirring occasionally to prevent sticking. Check seasoning.

Nutty Noodles

2	onions, chopped	½ c	dry soybeans, cooked
½ c	butter	⅔ c	peanut butter
1½ c	Granola	2 c	yogurt
1 c	peanuts	1 t	nutmeg, ground
12 oz	whole-wheat noodles, cooked		

Sauté onions briefly in the butter. Add Granola and peanuts, and stir until onions and peanuts are lightly browned. Mix with the noodles and soybeans in a casserole and place in a 350° oven until heated. Transfer to a serving dish. Blend together the peanut butter, yogurt, and nutmeg, and stir into noodle mixture. Season with salt and pepper.

Trudy's Danish Noodle Pudding

2 c noodles, crushed	¼ lb butter, melted
1 T sea salt	2 eggs, beaten
boiling water	1 T butter
3 oz cream cheese	1 c Granola, ground
1 c sour cream	3 T honey
¼ c honey	1 t cinnamon, ground

Cook noodles in boiling, salted water until almost done. Drain but do not rinse. Put into deep bowl. Soften and cream the cream cheese. Beat in sour cream, honey, melted butter, and beaten eggs. Blend well into drained noodles. Line low, flat casserole with aluminum foil and oil well. Add noodle mixture. Make topping: melt butter in frypan, add Granola, honey, and cinnamon. Stir well but do not cook. Spread over noodle pudding. Bake 30 to 40 minutes at 350°, until set.

CHAPTER 8

SALADS AND DRESSINGS USING GRANOLA

Salads and salad dressings are probably *the* most unexpected places to find Granola. But think about it again. Salads are often made with fruits, and Granola fits fine there. Or vegetables, again appropriate. Or bits of meat— why not? What's so unexpected? As for the dressings, Granola ground in an electric blender affords them a little texture and an earthier taste.

The salads come first, in an approximate order of ones featuring meat, vegetables, then fruit. Chicken salad is present, and potato, coleslaw, deviled egg, Caesar, macaroni —and some more inventive ones.

The dressings follow, and with ground Granola in them, they are not the most usual. There is sesame, East Indian, cucumber, sweet-and-sour, and so on. Oh, and French.

Something to think about: Using both a Granola dressing and a Granola salad might be too much at once, even for the Granola connoisseur.

SALADS

Chicken Salad with Granola

3 c cooked chicken, diced	¾ c mayonnaise
1½ c celery, chopped	1 T parsley, chopped
2 T onion, minced	½ t sea salt
½ c Granola	¼ t ground pepper
¼ c chicken stock	lettuce

Combine the chicken, celery, onion, and Granola. Mix together the stock, mayonnaise, and seasonings, and stir into the salad. Serve on lettuce.

Ham and Granola Salad

2 c cooked ham, diced	⅓ c sour cream
1½ c celery, diced	¼ c black olives, pitted
2 T vinegar	and halved
2 T honey	2 c Granola
½ c mayonnaise	1 c Swiss cheese, grated

Marinate ham and celery in mixed vinegar and honey for one hour in refrigerator. Stir in mayonnaise and sour cream. Pour mixture into pan and chill. Sprinkle with olives. Combine cheese and Granola and spread on top. Broil until cheese melts.

Spinach-Bacon-Granola Salad

2 lbs spinach, cooked and dried	8 slices bacon, cooked and crumbled
3 hard-boiled eggs, shelled and chopped	1 T lemon juice
¼ c Granola	1 T honey
	1 T vegetable oil

Shred spinach and add eggs, Granola, and bacon. Blend lemon juice, honey, and oil and sprinkle over.

African Salad

1 head lettuce, shredded	1 c baked beans, drained
4 green onions, chopped	¼ c Granola
1 potato, boiled and sliced	1 c salmon, cooked and shredded
6 radishes, minced	2 hard-boiled eggs, shelled and sliced
1 cucumber, peeled and sliced thinly	2 tomatoes, sliced
	½ c mayonnaise
	⅓ c coconut milk

Layer on a platter, from bottom up: lettuce, onions, potato, radishes, cucumber, beans, Granola, salmon, eggs, tomatoes. Blend mayonnaise and coconut milk, and pour over salad.

Potato Granola Salad

2 T consommé	8 potatoes (with skins), cooked and diced
1 c mayonnaise	
¼ c wine vinegar	
4 hard-boiled eggs, shelled and chopped	5 green onions, minced
1 T tarragon, ground	1 c celery, diced
2 T parsley, chopped	4 radishes, minced
1 T sea salt	½ c pickles, minced
1 T ground pepper	1 c Granola

Blend consommé, mayonnaise, and vinegar, and stir in eggs and seasonings. Separately, mix together the potatoes, onion, celery, radishes, pickles, and Granola. Pour first mixture over second and toss gently but thoroughly.

Granola Coleslaw

Coleslaw is crunchy. Granola coleslaw is even crunchier.

½ cabbage head, shredded	2 T vinegar
	2 T Granola
1 carrot, grated	1 T dill seeds
⅓ c yogurt	½ t sea salt
⅓ c sour cream	½ t paprika
2 T honey	

Combine cabbage and carrot. Combine other ingredients separately. Stir dressing into cabbage mixture.

Caesar Salad with Granola

Granola serves as croutons here.

1	garlic clove	¼ c	Parmesan cheese, grated
1 t	sea salt		
⅛ t	cayenne, ground	1	small can anchovies, drained and crushed
1 t	mustard powder		
2 T	lemon juice	1	egg, boiled one minute
¼ c	vegetable oil		
1	large head Romaine lettuce (or 2 small heads)	¾ c	Granola

Rub bowl with garlic. Add and stir together the salt, cayenne, mustard, and lemon juice. Blend oil in. Wash and dry lettuce well and tear into pieces. Add to bowl. Sprinkle on cheese and anchovies. Break egg over salad. Sprinkle with Granola, and toss.

String Bean, Beet, and Granola Salad

¼ c	wine vinegar	2 c	string beans, broken and cooked
1 t	prepared mustard		
1½ t	sea salt	1 c	beets, cooked and sliced
½ t	ground pepper		
¼ c	vegetable oil	¼ c	Granola

Mix vinegar, mustard, salt, and pepper. Stir oil in. Add string beans and beets. Pour Granola over and serve.

Granola Vegetable Salad

½ c	cooked potatoes, diced	1	stalk celery, diced
1 c	beets, cooked and diced	1	green pepper, diced
		4	green onions, chopped
¼ c	cabbage, grated	½ c	apples, cored and diced
¼ c	carrots, grated	⅓ c	Granola

Mix all ingredients and serve.

Macaroni and Granola Salad

1 lb whole-wheat or wheat-
      soy elbow macaroni,
      cooked
½ c Granola
2 T green onions,
      chopped
2 T celery, diced

⅛ t nutmeg, ground
1 t sea salt
¼ t ground pepper
¼ c mayonnaise
2 T vegetable oil
2 T vinegar
2 T honey

Combine all ingredients; serve.

Granola Deviled Egg Salad

6   hard-boiled eggs,
      shelled
¼ t green onions, minced
2 T butter
2 T mayonnaise

1 T Granola, ground
⅛ t curry powder
½ t sea salt
¼ t ground pepper
lettuce

Halve the eggs; remove and mash the yolks. Sauté the green onions in butter for a couple of minutes, and stir with the mayonnaise, Granola, curry powder, salt, pepper and yolks. Stuff this mixture into the egg whites. Serve on lettuce.

Bean Sprout Treat Salad

2   stalks celery, chopped
3 T Granola
¼ lb bean sprouts
½ t caraway seeds

lettuce
1 T honey
2 T lemon juice

Mix celery, Granola, bean sprouts, and caraway seeds. Turn out on a lettuce-lined plate. Blend honey with lemon juice and dribble over salad.

Avocado-Granola Salad with Orange

1	head lettuce	¼ c	Granola
2	avocados, peeled and	1 t	lemon juice
	sliced	1 T	vegetable oil
1 c	orange sections		

Shred lettuce and add avocados, orange sections, and Granola. Mix and sprinkle on the lemon juice and oil. Toss.

Crunchy Cottage Cheese Salad

1 c	bean sprouts	2	green onions,
¼	cucumber, peeled		chopped finely
	and sliced	¼ c	Granola
4	radishes, minced	½ c	cottage cheese

Mix all ingredients together and serve.

Salad with Chicory and Granola

½ lb	chicory (or endive)	2 T	vegetable oil
½ c	dried apricots, soaked	¼ t	sea salt
	and chopped	⅛ t	ground pepper
3	pears, cored and	¼ t	marjoram, ground
	diced	2 T	vinegar
1 c	Granola		

Tear chicory into bite-sized pieces. Stir in the apricots, pears, and Granola. Toss with oil, add seasonings, and toss again with vinegar.

Granola-Pineapple Salad

2 c	Granola (with	2 T	mint tea leaves,
	coconut)		crushed
1	pineapple, skinned	2 c	yogurt
	and cubed	⅛ t	honey
5	apples, cored and		
	cubed		

Mix together the Granola, pineapple, and apples. Combine the mint, yogurt, and honey, and stir into the salad.

Fresh Fruit and Granola Salad

1 c strawberries, stemmed and quartered	1 c peaches, pitted and sliced
1 c bananas, skinned, sliced and tossed with lemon juice	1 c pears, cored and sliced
	1 c Granola

Mix all ingredients and serve.

Om Salad
A lot of juicy melon for a big summer celebration.

1 canteloupe	2 c Granola
1 honeydew melon	¼ c ginger, ground
1 watermelon	¼ c cinnamon, ground
1 c shredded coconut	

Remove seeds and cube the meat of the melons. Mix melon cubes, Granola, and coconut. Combine seasonings and sprinkle on.

Granola-Peach Spicy Salad

⅓ c vinegar	1 T ginger, ground
¼ c water	4 peaches, halved and pitted
⅓ c honey	
1 T cinnamon, ground	lettuce
1 T cloves, ground	1 c Granola

In a saucepan, simmer the vinegar, water, honey, and spices for five minutes. Pour onto the peaches, and chill. Prepare for serving by draining peach halves and placing them (hollow-side-up) on lettuce. Fill peach cavities with Granola.

Fruit and Celery Salad with Granola

3 apples, cored and
   chopped
3 stalks celery, diced
1 banana, peeled and
   diced

⅓ c Granola
¼ c yogurt
¼ c mayonnaise

Stir together the apples, celery, banana, and Granola. Mix yogurt and mayonnaise and blend into salad.

Heavy Fruit Salad

1½ c yogurt
1 c sour cream
½ c dates, pitted and
   chopped

½ c raisins
½ c figs, chopped
½ c shredded coconut
½ c Granola

Combine yogurt and sour cream and mix in other ingredients.

Granola Salad

2½ c Granola
1 apple, cored and
   chopped

½ c dates, pitted and
   chopped
1 head lettuce,
   shredded

Mix ingredients. Serve with French dressing.

Apple and Granola Salad

4 apples, cored and
   grated

2 c Granola
½ t nutmeg, ground

Mix and serve.

SALAD DRESSINGS

French Dressing with Granola

⅓ c wine vinegar   ¼ t ground pepper
3 T Granola, ground   1 c vegetable oil
¾ t sea salt

Stir together the vinegar, Granola, salt, and pepper, then gradually add the oil.

Sour Granola Dressing

3 T lemon juice   ½ t sea salt
2 T wine vinegar   ⅛ t ground pepper
3 T Granola, ground   ½ c vegetable oil
¼ t dry mustard

Combine all ingredients except oil. Then add oil slowly.

Sweet-and-Sour Fruit Dressing with Granola

2 T orange juice   ½ t ginger, ground
2 T lemon juice   ½ t sea salt
2 T Granola, ground   ⅔ c vegetable oil

Mix together all ingredients except oil. Then beat in the oil slowly.

East India Dressing

⅓ c wine vinegar   3 T Granola, ground
2 T chutney, chopped   ¾ t sea salt
1 t curry powder   ¼ t ground pepper
⅛ t cumin, ground   ¾ c vegetable oil

Blend together all ingredients except oil; then gradually mix oil in.

Sesame Granola Dressing

2 T sesame seeds
1 garlic clove, minced
   or crushed
½ c sesame oil

3 T lemon juice
3 T Granola, ground
¼ t sea salt

Sauté sesame seeds and garlic in oil briefly. Cool. Combine with remaining ingredients.

Spanish Dressing

1 sharp chili pepper
3 garlic cloves
½ c vegetable oil
¼ c wine vinegar

¼ c Granola
¾ t sea salt
¼ c black olives, pitted
     and chopped

Blend all ingredients (except olives) together in electric blender. Stir in olives.

Cucumber Dressing

½ c cucumber, peeled
     and diced
3 T Granola
⅓ c buttermilk
3 T mayonnaise

1 T lemon juice
½ t garlic, minced
¼ t sea salt
⅛ t ground pepper

Blend all ingredients in electric blender; chill.

Cheese Dressing

¼ c Parmesan cheese,
     grated
2 T Granola, ground

1 c mayonnaise
2 t tamari

Combine all ingredients.

Lemon Granola Dressing

3 T lemon juice	1 c yogurt
2 T honey	3 T Granola, ground

Mix all ingredients thoroughly.

Eastern Dressing

2 c mayonnaise	½ t ginger, ground
¼ c Granola, ground	¼ t curry powder
1 T sesame seeds	¼ t nutmeg, ground
1 T currants	

Mix all ingredients.

CHAPTER 9

GRANOLA AND FRUIT

We regret that fruits, with their sweet, distinct flavors and moist textures do not naturally make up main courses. Their dishes do add a special extra character to a meal, however, and are well worth inclusion. Baked, fried, steamed, creamed, or whatever, most fruit dishes are on the sweet side, and Granola complements well here—and contrasts pleasantly in texture.

When it comes to fruit recipes, there's no great reason to feel bound by the rules. Use what's in season, if you like.

Incidentally, more fruit recipes are available in the salad chapter.

Fried Granola Apples

6 apples	¼ c date sugar
2 T butter	⅛ t sea salt
¾ c Granola	

Core and quarter apples. Slice thinly and put in hot frying pan with butter. Turn often, browning well. Add re-

115

maining ingredients a few moments before apples are brown and tender.

Fried Banana-Granola Balls

6   bananas   1 c vegetable oil
3 c Granola, ground

Peel and mash bananas. Mix ground Granola in. Mold this dough into small balls. Heat oil and drop balls in it individually to brown.

Honey-Baked Granola Pears

6   pears, halved and   ½ c Granola
    cored   1 t ginger, ground
¼ c lemon juice   2 T vegetable oil
¼ c honey   1 t cloves, ground

Set pears in oiled casserole. Combine lemon juice, honey, ginger, Granola, oil, and cloves, and pour over fruit. Bake at 350° for 15 minutes.

Laurie's Idea

1¼ c Granola   1   cantaloupe (meat
 ½ c honey   diced)
 2 T butter   ½ lb peaches, pitted and
 2 t cinnamon, ground   quartered
 1 c blackberries

Mix Granola, honey, butter, and cinnamon and spread two-thirds of it in oiled casserole. Cover with fruit. Sprinkle remainder of Granola mixture on top. Bake at 375° for 30 minutes.

Granola Banana Bites

1 c Granola   6   bananas
¼ c honey

Combine Granola and honey. Peel bananas, cut into one-inch lengths, and roll in Granola. Chill.

Berries and Granola Extra

½ c yogurt   stemmed and
½ c mayonnaise   quartered
¼ c honey   ½ c raspberries
1 t vanilla extract   ½ c boysenberries
½ c strawberries,   ½ c Granola

Blend yogurt, mayonnaise, honey, and vanilla. Mix fruit and Granola in. Chill.

Crunchy Fruit Cream

1 pt sour cream   ½ c raisins
1 c   pineapple, crushed   1 c Granola
1 c   strawberries, stemmed ½ c honey
2   oranges, peeled and
      sectioned

Stir together all ingredients. Cool a few hours before serving.

Granola Spiced Fruit

1 c apple juice   1 c oranges, peeled and
½ c vinegar   sectioned
½ c date sugar   1 c apricots, pitted and
¼ c honey   quartered
2 T cinnamon, ground   1 c blueberries
1 T cloves, ground   1 c Granola
1 T allspice, ground

Simmer together for five minutes the apple juice, vinegar, sugar, honey, and spices. Add fruit and simmer five additional minutes. Chill, then stir in Granola.

Granola Applesauce

2 lbs apples	1 c Granola
boiling water	1 t cinnamon, ground
¼ c honey	

Quarter apples and remove cores. Put into saucepan with just enough boiling water to cover. Boil until mushy, adding water to keep from going dry. Stir in honey, Granola, and cinnamon.

Granola Plumsauce

2 lbs plums	¼ c honey
½ c boiling water	½ c Granola

Slice plums in half and remove pits. Put into saucepan with boiling water; boil for about 15 minutes. Press through colander or food mill. Mix in honey and Granola.

Steamed Pears with Granola

6 pears	1 T ginger, ground
2 T boiling water	¼ c date sugar
¾ c Granola (approx.)	

Core pears from blossom end. Put into saucepan with boiling water. Steam eight minutes or until tender. Mix ginger into Granola. Stuff pears with Granola and sprinkle with the date sugar. Chill.

Stuffed Figs

1 lb figs   ¾ c Granola
2 T boiling water   ¼ c honey

Place figs in saucepan with boiling water and cover until plump. Mix Granola and honey. Slit each fig and stuff with Granola.

Cranberries Granola

1½ lbs cranberries   ½ c honey
  2 T boiling water   ½ c Granola

Put cranberries and boiling water into saucepan over low heat and cover. Steam 18 minutes. Chill, then stir in honey and Granola.

CHAPTER 10

GRANOLA BREADS, MUFFINS, AND SPREADS

Exotic, offbeat breads are not the only possibilities here for utilizing Granola. In this chapter, you will find such old standards as whole-wheat, rye, potato, cracked wheat, brown bread, and cornbread, separated into Yeast Breads and Non-Yeast Breads sections. Granola simply adds a gentle crunchiness to any bread, perhaps a sweetness, a nuttiness. Almost any loaf could benefit from the addition of Granola.

The breads are followed by Muffins and Such. As with the breads, so with the muffins. Granola fits. And the places it fits are varied. Besides muffins, there are rolls, sticks, croquettes, crackers, bagels, doughnuts, and more.

And then come the spreads to put on the muffins and breads. Now, *they* are exotic.

YEAST BREADS

Whole-Wheat Bread with Granola
Richly wheaty, crunchy and sweet, and not too heavy.

1 c warm water	3 c whole-wheat flour
1½ T yeast	(approx.), at room
⅓ c honey	temperature
1 egg, at room	1 t sea salt
temperature	1 c Granola

Sprinkle yeast into warm water and let stand five minutes. Then break in egg, add honey, and beat vigorously until frothy and full of air. Add 1½ cups flour, stirring, to make a batter consistency. Let sit 20 minutes in warm place to rise. (This step will lighten the final product.) Then add the salt and Granola and mix in, and keep stirring in flour until the dough is too stiff to stir. Cover board with flour and knead dough, at first adding flour regularly to stiffen a little more and to counter the stickiness. Knead until the bread resists kneading; put into bowl, cover with towel, and leave to rise for one hour in a warm place. Knead again, punch into oiled bread pan, and let rise another hour. Bake in 350° oven for 50 minutes. Remove from pan and let cool on wire rack.

Granola Bread

1 c warm milk	1½ c Granola
2 T yeast	2¼ c whole-wheat pastry
2 T honey	flour
2 T butter	

Mix the milk, yeast, and honey and let sit for 15 minutes. Add the butter and Granola and beat in, then mix in the flour. Knead and let rise for an hour. Knead and shape into oiled bread pan. Let rise 40 minutes. (If you like, for decoration, brush top with egg white and sprinkle on a little Granola.) Bake at 375° for 45 to 50 minutes.

Rye Granola Bread

1 T yeast	1 t fennel, ground
1 T date sugar	1 T caraway seeds
¼ c lukewarm water	2 c rye flour
1 c warm scalded milk	1 c whole-wheat flour
¼ c molasses	¾ c Granola (with rye
2 T butter	flakes)
1 T sea salt	

Melt the yeast and sugar in the lukewarm water. Add the milk, molasses, butter, fennel, and caraway. Combine the flours and Granola and stir into the first mixture. Knead; let rise for an hour. Knead and press into oiled bread pan; let rise 45 minutes. Bake at 350° for 55 minutes.

Granola Potato Bread

1	large potato	½ c	powdered milk
⅓ c	hot water	2	eggs, beaten
1 T	yeast	2 c	whole-wheat pastry
¼ c	warm milk		flour
½ c	honey	1 c	Granola
⅓ c	butter	1½ t	cardamon, ground
1 T	sea salt		

Dice potato, add the water, cover, and cook over a low flame. Meanwhile, dissolve the yeast in the milk and honey, and let sit. Mix the butter, salt, and powdered milk. Once the potato is tender, sieve it, undrained, into the butter mixture (the ingredients will melt), and stir until smooth, adding the yeast mixture and the eggs. Then beat in the flour, Granola, and cardamon, and continue beating for a few minutes. Cover and let rise. Knead, form into oiled bread pan and let rise again. Bake for 55 minutes at 350°.

Cracked Wheat Granola Bread

1 c	warm water	1 t	sea salt
1 T	yeast	¾ c	cracked wheat
⅓ c	honey	½ c	Granola (with wheat
1	egg		flakes)
2¼ c	whole-wheat flour		

Follow directions for the Whole-Wheat Bread with Granola recipe (pp. 120–121), adding the cracked wheat with the Granola.

Pumpernickle-Granola Bread

2 T yeast	2 t sea salt
¼ c lukewarm water	¾ c buckwheat flour
¼ c molasses	¾ c rye flour
3 T butter	1½ c whole-wheat flour
1 c hot water	¾ c molasses Granola

Mix the yeast, water, and molasses until it is frothy. Let the butter melt in the water. Stir in the yeast mixture. Combine the flours and Granola and stir the yeast-butter in. Beat hard for several minutes, adding warm water if necessary. Cover and let rise in a warm place. Knead, shape dough into an oiled bread pan, and let rise again. Bake for 50 minutes at 350°.

Cheese Bread with Granola

1 c warm water	⅛ c butter
2 T yeast	½ t sea salt
⅛ c honey	⅔ c Granola
1 egg	1 c Cheddar cheese,
2 c whole-wheat flour	grated

Begin as with the Whole-Wheat Bread with Granola recipe (pp. 120–121), but leave the batter-consistency mixture to rise for 20 minutes. Then add the butter, salt, and Granola and mix in, followed by the cheese. Stir in flour until the dough is too stiff to stir, and follow the Whole-Wheat Bread recipe again to the end.

Nut-Raisin Granola Bread

1 T yeast	1 t sea salt
2 c warm water	1 t cinnamon, ground
½ c molasses	2 c Granola
6½ c whole-wheat flour	1 c raisins
½ c vegetable oil	1 c walnuts, broken
1 egg	

Mix yeast in water; let stand a few minutes. Add molasses and 2 cups flour; blend well. Cover and let rise in warm place for 20 minutes. Add remaining ingredients and blend well, using enough flour to make dough stiff. Cover and let rise, then punch down. Shape into two loaves, place in oiled bread pans, and let rise. Bake at 350° for one hour.

Granola Banana Bread

1 T yeast	1 c whole-wheat flour
⅛ c warm apple cider or juice	¾ c Granola
	¼ t sea salt
2 T honey	¼ t fennel seeds, ground
2 T vegetable oil	½ c mashed bananas
2 eggs, beaten	

Let yeast sit in cider a few moments. Mix honey, oil, and eggs, and add to yeast mixture. Stir in flour, Granola, salt, and fennel. Let rise for a half-hour, covered and warm. Mix in bananas. Form into oiled bread pan. Let rise 30 minutes, and bake for 40 minutes at 325°.

Cinnamon Swirl Granola Bread
Granola makes this perennial favorite even better.

1 c warm water	1 t sea salt
1 T yeast	1 c Granola
⅓ c honey	¼ c cinnamon, ground
1 egg	¼ c date sugar
2½ c whole-wheat pastry flour	

Follow recipe for Whole-Wheat Bread with Granola (pp. 120–121), until it is time to form the dough into the pan. Instead, roll it out into a rectangle. Mix the cinnamon and date sugar (and ⅛ cup more Granola, if you like) and sprinkle over the dough. Then roll it up, tightly; pinch the loose ends sealed. Place in an oiled bread pan and let rise, following again the Whole-Wheat Bread recipe to the end.

Granola Millet Bread

1 c warm water	2¼ c whole-wheat flour
1 T yeast	1 t sea salt
¼ c honey	¾ c cracked millet
1 egg	½ c Granola

Prepare as for the Whole-Wheat Bread with Granola recipe (pp. 120–121), adding the millet with the Granola.

Buttermilk Granola Bread

1 T yeast	3 c whole-wheat pastry
2 T date sugar	flour
⅓ c warm water	1 c Granola
¼ c butter, softened	2½ t sea salt
1 c buttermilk, warmed	1 T caraway, ground

Put the yeast and sugar in the water and let sit for a few minutes. Add the butter and buttermilk. Mix the flour, Granola, salt, and caraway; make a well in the center, and mix in the liquids. Beat hard for a couple of minutes, making a spongy dough. Cover and let rise in a warm place for one hour. Beat down, mold into an oiled bread pan, and let rise again. Bake 50 minutes in a 350° oven.

Granola Sunflower Bread

2 T yeast	1 T vegetable oil
2 c warm water	1 c sunflower seeds
2 c Granola	5 c whole-wheat flour
½ t sea salt	

Let the yeast sit for a few minutes in the water. Add the Granola, and mix in the other ingredients. Let rise, covered, in a warm place. Knead, divide in two, and mold into two oiled bread pans. Let rise again. Bake for one hour at 350°.

Fruit Bread with Granola

2 T yeast	5½ c whole-wheat pastry
1½ c warm milk	flour
⅔ c honey	1½ c dried fruits, chopped
1 T butter	1½ c Granola
1 t sea salt	date sugar
1 egg	water

Let the yeast sit in the warm milk for five minutes. Add the honey, butter, salt, and egg, and beat. Mix in 5 cups of the flour. Dredge the fruit in the remaining ½ cup of the flour, add the Granola, and combine these into the dough. Cover the dough and allow to rise in a warm place for two or three hours. Knead, divide in two, form into oiled bread pans, and let rise for at least one hour. Bake for 40 minutes at 350°. Remove from oven and pan, glaze with a thick mixture of date sugar and water, and set on cooling rack.

NON-YEAST BREADS

Granola Boston Brown Bread

1 c whole-wheat flour	2 t baking soda
1 c rye flour	1 t sea salt
1 c Granola (one with	1 c molasses
raisins)	2 c buttermilk
1 c corn meal	¾ c raisins

Mix the flours, Granola, corn meal, baking soda, and salt. Combine separately the molasses, buttermilk, and raisins, and mix into the dry ingredients. Oil two or three cans (one-lb. coffee cans are a good size), fill with the dough, and cover with can lids and aluminum foil. Set upright in large pans filled with water halfway up the sides of the cans. Cover and bake for three hours, adding more water if needed.

Granola Cornbread

2 c corn meal	4 c buttermilk
½ c Granola	4 eggs
1 t sea salt	

Blend all ingredients in electric blender until you have a smooth batter. Pour this into two oiled bread pans and bake for 30 minutes at 400°.

Heavy Granola Loaf

6 c whole-wheat flour	1 t tamari
4 c Granola	¼ c vegetable oil

Mix ingredients and form into oiled bread pan. Let sit overnight, covered with damp towel. Bake at 350° for 80 minutes, until dark brown.

Date-Granola Bread

1 c dates, pitted and chopped	1 t vanilla extract
½ t sea salt	1½ c honey
2½ T butter	2 c whole-wheat flour
1 c boiling water	1½ t baking soda
1 egg	½ t baking powder
	1½ c Granola

Mix dates, salt, and butter, cover with boiling water, and let stand ten minutes. Meanwhile blend the egg, vanilla, and honey. Sift together the flour, baking soda, and baking powder, and stir in the Granola. Mix the date and egg combinations, then add this to the flour one and beat thoroughly. Place in two oiled bread pans and bake at 375° for 45 minutes, until the top cracks.

Crunchy Bread

1 T butter	2 t baking powder
1 c honey	¾ c milk
1 egg	1 c Granola (one with
2 c whole-wheat flour	nuts)
1 t sea salt	

Cream the butter and honey and beat in egg. Stir together the flour, salt, and baking powder. Slowly add the flour mixture and the milk alternately to the creamed butter. Beat until smooth. Mix in the Granola. Pour into an oiled bread pan and bake at 325° for 75 minutes.

Naomi's Hobo Bread

A bread good enough to make friends with.

2 c raisins	3 c whole-wheat flour
2½ c water	1 c Granola
4 t baking soda	1 egg
1 c honey	1 c sunflower seeds
½ t sea salt	1 c shredded coconut

Soak raisins overnight in water and baking soda. The next day, mix other ingredients together and stir in raisins and raisin water. Oil and flour empty coffee cans and fill half-full with dough. Bake one hour at 350° or until a stick of spaghetti comes out clean. Cool before removing from can. (For an almond-date variety, substitute 1 cup each of dates and almonds for the sunflower seeds and coconut, and add 2 tsp. almond extract.)

African Banana Loaf with Granola

2 c Granola	2 eggs, beaten
4 t baking powder	½ c honey
1 t nutmeg, ground	1 c vegetable oil
½ t sea salt	1 c water
1½ c mashed bananas	

Combine the Granola, baking powder, nutmeg, and salt. Slowly stir in the other ingredients. Bake in an oiled bread pan for 50 minutes at 350°.

Orange Marmalade Granola Bread

½ c honey	1½ c whole-wheat flour
2 T butter	1 T baking powder
3 eggs, beaten	1 t sea salt
1 c orange marmalade	1 c Granola

Cream honey, butter, and eggs. Blend in marmalade. Sift flour, baking powder, and salt together. Add flour mixture and Granola to egg mixture and stir. Spread into an oiled bread pan. Bake 55 minutes at 350°. Cool in pan for five minutes, then remove and cool on wire rack.

MUFFINS AND SUCH

Granola Whole-Wheat Rolls

1 T yeast	2½ c whole-wheat flour
1 c warm water	2 egg whites
1 T honey	1 c Granola
1½ t sea salt	1 egg yolk
2 T vegetable oil	1 T water

Combine the yeast, water, and honey and let sit a few minutes. Add the salt, oil, and 1 cup flour; stir until smooth. Beat the egg whites until stiff and add to batter. Now add the Granola and remaining flour. Knead a few minutes, then let rise an hour in a covered bowl in a warm place. Knead again, cover, and let rise 15 minutes. Knead, separate into 18 pieces, and form each into a ball. Touch the bottoms in corn meal and set on oiled cookie sheet, 1½ inches apart. Cover and allow to rise for 50 minutes. Beat the egg yolk and water together and brush each roll. Bake rolls at 400° for 18 minutes.

Cracked Wheat Granola Rolls

½ c	cracked wheat	½ c	honey
1 c	cold water	¼ c	vegetable oil
½ t	sea salt	2 t	sea salt
1 T	yeast	4 c	whole-wheat flour
¼ c	warm water	2 c	Granola
1½ c	scalded milk	butter	
1	egg		

For several hours, soak cracked wheat in cold water and salt. Begin actual preparation by letting yeast sit in the warm water for a few minutes. Then mix in (one ingredient at a time) the milk, egg, honey, oil, and finally salt. Add the cracked wheat and its water. Mix in the flour and Granola. Knead the dough; let it rise. Knead it again, roll it out, and cut out whatever shapes you would like to try for rolls—about 30. Arrange on an oiled baking sheet. Let rise, and brush the tops with melted butter. Bake at 375° for 15 minutes.

Whole-Wheat Granola Buns

1 T	yeast	2½ c	whole-wheat flour
1 c	milk, scalded	1 t	sea salt
3 T	honey	1 t	cinnamon, ground
¼ c	vegetable oil	¾ c	Granola
1	egg yolk		

Allow yeast to sit in the milk for a few minutes. Beat in honey, oil, and egg yolk. Sift flour, salt, and cinnamon together and add. Stir in Granola. Cover and let rise in a warm place until double in size. Knead and shape into about 20 small balls. Place on oiled baking pan. Let rise again. Brush with diluted honey to glaze. Bake at 400° for 30 minutes.

Granola Muffins

2 eggs, separated	1½ c milk
1 t sea salt	1½ c whole-wheat flour
1 t honey	1½ c Granola
½ c vegetable oil	

Beat egg yolks until thick, and add salt, honey, and oil. Stir in milk, flour, and Granola thoroughly. Beat egg whites until stiff, and fold in. Bake in hot, oiled muffin pans at 350° for 40 minutes. Makes 18 muffins.

Granola Energy Muffins

Folks who have eaten these innocent-looking muffins say they have experienced a noticeable burst of energy a few minutes later.

2½ c Granola	1 t sea salt
1 c whole-wheat flour	2½ t baking powder
¼ c soy flour	½ c vegetable oil
¾ c wheat germ	1 c molasses
½ c powdered milk	1½ c milk
½ c sesame seeds, ground	2 eggs
½ c brewer's yeast	

Stir together Granola, flours, wheat germ, powdered milk, sesame seeds, brewer's yeast, salt, and baking powder. Blend the oil, molasses, milk, and eggs; mix into dry ingredient. Bake in oiled muffin tins for 18 minutes at 375°.

Orange Granola Muffins

These muffins are on the sweet side and go well with light meals.

1½ c whole-wheat flour	½ c yogurt
¾ c Granola	¼ c vegetable oil
2 t baking powder	½ c honey
½ t sea salt	2 T orange peel, grated
1 egg, beaten	

Stir together flour, Granola, baking powder, and salt. Mix egg, yogurt, oil, honey, and orange peel. Add the liquid mixture to the dry ingredients and stir just enough to moisten. Bake at 375° for 20 minutes, in oiled muffin tins.

Granola Date Gems

1 c honey
½ c vegetable oil
2 c eggs, beaten
½ t sea salt
1 c milk
2 c whole-wheat flour

1 c Granola (one with dried fruits)
1 c dates, pitted and chopped
1 T powdered fruit rind

Beat together honey, oil, and eggs; add salt and milk. Stir together and mix in the other ingredients. Fill oiled, hot gem pans two-thirds full. Bake for 32 minutes at 350°.

Granola Sticks

Versatile: serve with lunches or a soup, or for party treats, or kids' snacks.

1¼ c milk
1 T honey
½ c vegetable oil

2 c whole-wheat flour
2 c Granola
1 t sea salt

Combine milk with honey and oil. Mix in remaining ingredients. Knead briefly. Roll out and cut into sticks, 1 inch by 3 inches each. Bake on oiled baking pan at 325° for 20 minutes, until lightly browned.

Granola-Date Sticks

1 c honey
2   eggs
3 c Granola, ground

1 c dates, pitted and chopped

Beat the honey and eggs together. Add the Granola and dates, and shape into thin sticks. Bake on oiled cookie sheet for ten minutes at 375°.

Granola Egg Bagels

1 c warm water	¼ c vegetable oil
1 T yeast	1 t sea salt
¼ c honey	1 c Granola
2 eggs, well beaten	1 c whole-wheat flour
2 c whole-wheat pastry	boiling water
flour	extra egg and topping

Mix the first five ingredients. Beat down and let rise. Then fold in the next four ingredients. Knead five minutes, and let rise 50 minutes. Knead and let rise half as long. Knead, cut into 24 pieces, and roll with hands into long round sticks. Connect ends of each to make into circles. Dunk these rings into boiling water for ten seconds. Place on oiled baking sheet. Brush with egg and, if you like, sprinkle with sesame or poppy seeds or Granola (perhaps ground). Let rise 20 minutes, and bake at 425° for 20 minutes.

Whole-Wheat Pizza Dough with Granola

1 c warm water	1 c Granola, ground
1 T baking powder	1 T chili powder
2 garlic cloves, minced	1 t sea salt
or crushed	1 t tarragon, ground
2 c whole-wheat flour	

Mix water, baking powder, and garlic and leave a few minutes. Then stir in 1 cup of the flour, the chili powder, salt, and tarragon. Add the Granola and remaining flour to make a firm, unsticking dough. Oil a baking sheet and press dough flat onto the center. Roll out with rolling pin and hands to cover entire pan evenly. Slice into eight sections now. Bake ten minutes in 350° oven to give an initial drying. (Otherwise, the middle part will remain moist.) Remove from oven and cover thoroughly with tomato sauce, spices, cheeses, meats, and whatever. Return to oven and bake 20 to 30 minutes more, until middle of dough is crisp enough to be picked up for eating.

Sesame Granola Crackers

1 c Granola, ground   1 T vegetable oil
¼ c sesame seeds   ⅞ c boiling water
½ t sea salt

Mix ingredients together. Drop into three-inch rounds on oiled cookie sheet. Bake until lightly browned at 400°.

Indian Fried Bread with Granola
An intriguing side-road adventure.

2 c whole-wheat flour   ½ c butter
1 c Granola   1 t sea salt
1½ c yogurt   vegetable oil

Stir all ingredients but oil together and knead until smooth. Roll by hands into balls, then flatten into thin cakes. Fry in hot oil until brown and puffed.

Walnut-Granola Croquettes

2 c Granola, ground   ¼ c parsley, chopped
1 c walnuts, ground   2   eggs, beaten
½ c Parmesan cheese,   ½ t sea salt
      grated   ¼ t savory, ground
4   green onions, minced   butter

Combine all ingredients except butter. Shape into patties and fry slowly in butter until crisp and brown.

Almond-Granola Curry Croquettes

2 c Granola, ground   2   eggs, beaten
1 c almonds, ground   1 t sea salt
8 oz cottage cheese   1 t curry powder
1   onion, minced   butter
1   clove garlic, minced

Combine all ingredients except butter. Shape into patties and fry slowly in butter until crisp and brown.

Chewy Granola-Meal Patties

1 c millet, uncooked
1 c cracked wheat,
     uncooked

2 c water
1 c Granola, ground
1 c walnuts, ground

Soak millet and cracked wheat overnight in water, then grind. Combine all ingredients. Form small patties and heat on dry griddle until brown on the outside but not cooked on the inside.

Granola Whole-Wheat Doughnuts

1 c honey
2   eggs, beaten
½ t sea salt
½ c sour cream
¾ c buttermilk

2 t baking powder
2 c whole-wheat flour
1 c Granola
vegetable oil
date sugar

Blend honey and eggs until thick and creamy. Add the salt, sour cream, buttermilk, and baking powder, then add flour and Granola. Roll dough ½-inch thick and cut with a doughnut cutter or into doughnut shape. Fry in deep oil at 375° until brown on both sides. Drain on paper towels and sprinkle with date sugar.

SPREADS

Granola Butter

¾ c Granola, ground
¼ c almonds, ground

¼ c vegetable oil
¼ c honey

Combine all ingredients. Use as you would peanut butter.

Chicken-Granola Spread

2 c cooked chicken,
     minced
¼ c celery, chopped finely

1   pimiento, chopped
     finely
½ c Granola, ground
     mayonnaise

Stir all ingredients together, adding enough mayonnaise to make a spreadable consistency.

Sweet Potato Granola Spread

1 c sweet potatoes,
    cooked and puréed
½ c shredded coconut

½ c Granola, ground
1 T vegetable oil

Mix all ingredients together.

Granola Cream Cheese Spread

¼ c Granola, ground
3 oz cream cheese

3 oz yogurt

Blend all ingredients together.

Pineapple-Granola Spread

3 oz cream cheese
¼ c Granola

¼ c pineapple chunks,
    puréed

Combine all ingredients.

Jane's Peanut Butter-Granola Spread

½ c Granola, ground
½ c peanut butter

½ c honey

Stir all together.

Crunchy Sour Peanut Spread

½ c Granola, ground
⅛ c sesame seeds

⅓ c peanut butter
⅓ c sour cream

Blend all ingredients.

Granola Applesauce Spread

½ c Granola, ground   ⅛ c honey
⅓ c applesauce

Combine these ingredients.

Date-Apple Granola Spread

½ c dates, pitted   ½ c Granola
1   apple, cored   ½ c honey

Blend ingredients together in an electric blender.

Date-Yogurt Granola Spread

1 c dates, pitted   ¼ c yogurt
½ c Granola (one with   ½ c powdered milk
     nuts)

Blend all ingredients in electric blender.

CHAPTER 11

COOKIES WITH GRANOLA

Besides breakfasts, cookies are the most traditional place to find Granola, which is very fitting. After all, what is Granola but cookie makings: oats, peanuts, raisins, honey, oil, flour, sesame seeds. You can take advantage of this fact yourself. Whatever your favorite cookie recipe is, you can almost surely substitute delicious, healthy Granola somewhere in it. If your recipe calls for a cup of oats, or coconut, try a cup of Granola, and you'll be delightfully surprised.

This chapter begins with a short section of recipes for cookies that feature Granola. Then will come the cookies that include Granola but have their own identifiable character. And they're all there: peanut butter cookies, fruit bars, brownies, sugar cookies, carob chip, meringues, macaroons, and more.

GRANOLA COOKIE RECIPES

Granola Cookies

3 c Granola, ground	½ c honey
1 c milk	

Heat Granola and milk in a covered saucepan over low heat for two minutes, being careful to avoid sticking. Uncover, and mix in the honey. Drop by spoonfuls onto an oiled cookie sheet and bake in a preheated 350° oven for 18 minutes. (Adding ½ cup shredded coconut and 1 tsp. almond extract will create a macaroon effect.)

Your Basic Cookie

1 c Granola	1 egg, beaten
¾ c whole-wheat flour	½ c butter
½ t sea salt	½ c honey
½ t baking soda	

Mix thoroughly, drop by spoonfuls onto an oiled cookie sheet, and bake at 350° for 12 minutes.

Ground Granola Cookies

2 c Granola, ground	½ t sea salt
2 c whole-wheat pastry flour	1¼ c honey
	1 c butter
½ t nutmeg, ground	¼ c buttermilk
1 t baking soda	

Add together the Granola, flour, nutmeg, baking soda, and salt. Cream the honey and butter, add the Granola mixture, and knead to form a soft dough, adding the buttermilk as needed. Roll out dough thinly and cut into large circles. Bake at 400° for ten minutes.

Granola Thins

½ c honey	¼ c whole-wheat flour
2 T butter	¼ c Granola, ground
1 egg	1 t baking powder
¼ c milk	¼ c Granola

Blend the honey, butter, egg, and milk. Stir together the flour, ground Granola, and baking powder, and slowly mix this into the honey mixture. Thinly spread this batter onto an oiled cookie sheet, sprinkle with the whole Granola, and bake at 350° for 18 minutes. When cool, cut into squares.

Granola Wafers

2 eggs	2 t baking powder
1 c honey	½ t sea salt
1 T butter	3 c Granola
1 t vanilla extract	

Beat the eggs for ten minutes. Add the honey, slowly, then the butter, vanilla, baking powder, salt, and Granola. Drop by small amounts onto an oiled cookie sheet and bake at 400° for ten minutes.

Granola Squares

1 egg, separated	3 T whole-wheat flour
⅓ c honey	⅛ t sea salt
¾ c Granola, ground coarsely	

Beat egg yolk until thick, and blend in the honey. Combine with Granola, flour, and salt, then fold in stiffly beaten egg white. Pour into oiled square pan. Bake at 350° for 22 minutes, until light brown. Cool and cut into squares.

COOKIE RECIPES WITH GRANOLA

New-Fashioned Sugar Cookies

2 eggs	2 c whole-wheat flour
1½ c date sugar	1½ c Granola, ground
1 c butter	½ t sea salt
1 T vanilla extract	2½ t baking powder

Beat together till fluffy the eggs, date sugar, butter, and vanilla. Sift together and add slowly the flour, Granola, salt, and baking powder, blending. Roll small balls of this dough, place on cookie sheet 2 inches apart, and flatten with the buttered bottom of a glass. Bake 10 to 12 minutes at 400°.

New Hampshire Ginger-Granola Cookies

3 c molasses	2 T ginger, ground
1 c butter	1 t cinnamon, ground
2 eggs	1½ t baking soda
¾ c sour cream	2½ c Granola, ground
2½ c whole-wheat flour	

Cream the molasses and butter; mix in the eggs, then the sour cream. Sift the flour, ginger, cinnamon, and soda into the ground Granola; stir. Mix the dry ingredients into the butter mixture, and knead into a smooth dough. Roll thin, cut into 2-inch circles, and bake at 350° until lightly browned.

Granola Meringues

Granola and date sugar combine here to give you the world's richest-flavored meringue.

2 egg whites	⅛ t sea salt
½ c date sugar	½ c Granola, ground
½ t vanilla extract	

Beat the egg whites until stiff. Continue beating steadily, and slowly add the date sugar. Add the vanilla, salt, and ground Granola now. Drop by spoonfuls onto a parchment-covered cookie sheet and bake at 275° for 20 minutes.

Gaye's Super Cookies

With a flavor admired by many. The ingredients and their amounts may be juggled to achieve a variety of delightful effects. Wheat germ, Granola, nuts, and oats need only be kept at a total of 4 cups.

2 eggs	2 c Granola
1 c butter or margarine	1 t baking soda
1 c brown sugar	1 c peanuts or walnuts
1 c flour	1½ c semi-sweet chocolate
1 c wheat germ	chips (optional)
½ t baking powder	1 t vanilla extract
½ t salt	

Beat eggs. Cream butter with brown sugar in bowl. Add eggs. Add other ingredients and mix well. Spoon onto cookie sheets and bake at 350° for about ten minutes.

Soft Granola Cookies

2½ c honey	½ t baking soda
½ c butter	1 t nutmeg, ground
4 eggs	1 t sea salt
1 c buttermilk	1½ c raisins
4 c whole-wheat flour	3½ c Granola

Cream the honey, butter, and eggs. Mix in the buttermilk and 2 cups of the flour alternately. Add the baking soda, nutmeg, salt, and raisins. Add the Granola, then the rest of the flour, and mix well. Drop in small amounts onto an oiled cookie sheet and bake at 450° for 14 minutes.

Coconut-Granola Macaroons

1 c Granola (one with almonds)	¾ c sweetened condensed milk
1⅔ c shredded coconut	½ t almond extract
1 egg, beaten	

Mix all the ingredients well and let stand briefly. Drop dough by teaspoonfuls onto parchment-covered cookie sheet. Bake in preheated 325° oven for 25 minutes. Remove from sheet immediately and cool on flat surface.

Granola-Date Macaroons

2½ c date sugar
 4   egg whites
 2 c Granola

1 c dates, pitted and
     chopped
½ t cinnamon, ground
1 t vanilla extract

Beat the sugar into the egg whites and continue until very stiff. Then add the Granola, dates, cinnamon, and vanilla. Drop by spoonfuls onto a parchment-covered cookie sheet and bake at 325° for 24 minutes.

Anise-Granola Macaroons

½ c honey
 4   egg whites, beaten
     stiff
 2 c Granola

1 c shredded coconut
½ t anise seeds, crushed
1 t sea salt

Blend the honey into the egg whites, and slowly add the rest of the ingredients as you continue stirring. Drop by teaspoonfuls onto an oiled baking sheet and bake for 20 minutes at 325°.

Carob Granola Brownies

½ c vegetable oil
½ c honey
 2   eggs, beaten
1 t vanilla extract

½ c carob powder
¼ t sea salt
 2 c whole-wheat flour
½ c Granola

Mix the oil and honey, then add the eggs and vanilla. Stir in the carob powder, salt, flour, and then Granola, in that order. Turn into an 8-inch square pan and bake for 30 minutes at 350°. When cool, cut into squares.

Carob-Pecan Granola Cookies

1 c butter	1 t baking soda
2¼ c honey	1 c carob powder
2 eggs	1 c Granola
3½ c whole-wheat flour	1 c pecans, chopped

Cream the butter, honey, and eggs until light. Sift together the flour, baking soda, and carob; add the Granola and pecans, and mix quickly into the butter mixture. Drop in small amounts onto an oiled baking sheet and bake at 425° until browned.

Granola-Chip Cookies

Just like good ol' chocolate chip, but healthier.

½ c vegetable oil	2 c whole-wheat flour
½ c honey	½ c Granola
½ t vanilla extract	½ c carob chips (or
2 eggs, beaten	chocolate)

Mix oil, honey, and vanilla, and beat in eggs. Then add flour, Granola, and carob chips, and blend well until stiff. Drop batter by teaspoonfuls onto oiled cookie sheet, and flatten cookies. Bake at 375° for ten minutes.

Banana Granola Cookies

½ c vegetable oil	½ c peanuts, ground
½ c honey	1½ c whole-wheat flour
1 egg	1 t sea salt
2 large bananas, peeled	¼ t nutmeg, ground
1¾ c Granola	¾ t cinnamon, ground

Blend oil, honey, egg, and bananas. Add to Granola and nuts, and combine with remaining ingredients to make a stiff batter. Drop by teaspoonfuls onto lightly oiled cookie sheet. Bake for 15 minutes at 400°.

Pineapple Granola Cookies

⅓ c vegetable oil   4 c Granola
⅔ c molasses   ½ c soy flour
  2   eggs   1 T baking yeast
½ c pineapple juice   ½ t sea salt
  1 t vanilla extract   ½ c pineapple bits

Blend oil and molasses, beat in eggs, and add the juice
and vanilla. Mix together the Granola, flour, yeast, salt, and
pineapple bits, and add this to the first mixture. Wait 30
minutes and then drop by spoonfuls onto oiled cookie sheet,
and bake at 375° for 13 minutes.

Granola Prune Bars

¼ c butter, melted   ¼ t sea salt
1½ c Granola   ½ t baking powder
  2   eggs   ¾ c prunes, pitted and
½ c date sugar   chopped
¾ c whole-wheat flour

Blend the butter and Granola. Press this mixture into an
oiled 8-inch square baking pan and refrigerate for 15 minutes. Beat the eggs and date sugar until creamy, then add the
vanilla. Mix the flour, salt, and baking powder, and stir into
the egg mixture. Add the prunes. Pour this batter into the
baking pan. (You might make another batch of the Granola-
butter mixture and add on top of the batter now.) Bake for
35 minutes at 350°, cool, and cut into bars.

Granola Fruit Squares

The fruits used are up to you.

⅔ c molasses   1 c whole-wheat flour
½ c vegetable oil   ⅛ t sea salt
  2 c Granola   2 c fruit, chopped

Blend the molasses and oil, and add the Granola, flour,
and salt. Press half of this mixture into an oiled 7- by 11-

inch pan. Spread over with the fruits. Then cover with the remaining dough. Bake for 25 minutes at 400°. Allow to cool, and cut into squares.

Coconut Granola Cookies

2   eggs, separated
½ c honey
1 c shredded coconut
2 c Granola, ground
½ c Granola
1 c dates, pitted and chopped
shredded coconut for rolling

Blend egg yolks and honey, then add coconut shreds, ground and whole Granola, and dates, mixing well. Fold in stiffly beaten egg whites, making a stiff dough. Roll into 1-inch balls and coat with extra coconut. Flatten each ball and arrange on oiled baking sheet. Bake at 325° for 17 minutes. Remove from sheet when completely cool.

Peanut Butter–Date Granola Cookies

½ c peanut butter
1 c honey
1 c butter
⅔ c date sugar
2   eggs
2 c whole-wheat flour
1 t sea salt
1 t cinnamon, ground
½ t nutmeg, ground
1 t baking powder
¼ t baking soda
2 c Granola, ground
1 c dates, pitted and chopped

Cream the peanut butter, honey, and butter, and stir in the date sugar until the mixture is fluffy. Beat the eggs in well. Sift the flour, salt, cinnamon, nutmeg, baking powder, and baking soda into the ground Granola, and blend slowly into the first mixture. Add the dates. Roll this dough by hand into four rolls that are 9 inches long. Wrap in waxed paper, place in refrigerator, and allow to chill thoroughly. Then slice thinly, place on an ungreased cookie sheet, and bake in a 400° oven for six minutes.

Munchy Peanut Butter Cookies

1 c honey	¼ t cloves, ground
½ c vegetable oil	½ t mace, ground
¾ c peanut butter	½ t sea salt
(crunchy)	2 t baking powder
2 eggs, beaten	1⅓ c Granola
1 t cinnamon, ground	¾ c ground Granola

Mix the honey and oil, then add the peanut butter and continue beating. Blend in eggs, cinnamon, cloves, mace, salt, and baking powder. Stir in the Granola, both whole and ground. Drop by spoonfuls onto an ungreased cookie sheet and bake at 325° for 12 minutes.

Sweet Rolled Granola

1¼ c Granola	½ t cinnamon, ground
½ c honey	½ t nutmeg, ground
½ c peanut butter	

Mix all of the ingredients together, roll by moistened hand into thin rolls about 3 inches long, and chill on waxed paper in the refrigerator. Serve.

Pecan-Granola Cookies

2 eggs, beaten	¼ c milk
½ c vegetable oil	1 c whole-wheat flour
½ c honey	1 c pecans, ground
½ t sea salt	1½ c Granola, ground
½ t fennel seeds, crushed	

Mix the eggs, oil, and honey, then add the salt, fennel, and milk. Stir in the flour, pecans, and Granola, making a stiff dough. Drop by spoonfuls onto an oiled baking sheet and bake at 350° for 15 minutes.

Walnut-Granola Cookies

4 eggs, separated	2 c Granola
½ c honey	1 c walnut pieces
½ c molasses	1 T cinnamon, ground
¾ c soy flour	

Blend the egg yolks, honey, and molasses, and add the other ingredients. Fold in the beaten egg whites. Spread onto an oiled baking sheet and bake for 20 minutes at 350°. When cool, cut into strips.

Granola-Walnut Wafers

A very thin, crunchy cookie.

2 eggs	⅛ t sea salt
1 c date sugar	½ c Granola
1 t walnut extract	½ c walnut pieces
3 T whole-wheat flour	

Beat the eggs for ten minutes, then add the date sugar and walnut extract and beat for three additional minutes. Sift together the flour and salt. Combine flour mixture, Granola, and walnuts with sugar mixture. Drop by small amounts onto oiled sheet and bake at 400° for five minutes.

Peanut-Granola Wafers

2 T butter	½ t baking soda
1 c honey	½ t sea salt
1 egg	½ c peanuts, ground
1 c whole-wheat flour	½ c Granola, ground

Blend the butter, honey, and egg. Sift together the flour, baking soda, and salt, and add these and the peanuts and Granola to the butter mixture. Spoon onto oiled baking sheet and bake at 400° until lightly browned.

Almond Granola Cakes

Granola goes Oriental in these flavorful morsels.

1 c rice flour	1½ c Granola
½ c date sugar	½ c butter, softened
1½ c almonds, chopped	½ t almond extract

Stir together the flour, date sugar, almonds, and Granola. Blend the butter and almond extract into this mixture, adding drops of water if needed to bind the dough. Roll by hand into small balls and bake at 350° until lightly browned.

Sesame Seed Cakes with Granola

2 eggs, beaten	½ t sea salt
½ c vegetable oil	1 orange rind, grated
½ c honey	1½ c whole-wheat flour
1 c sesame seeds	Granola
1 t cumin, ground	

Mix eggs, oil, and honey, then add seeds, rind, and salt. Stir in flour to make a stiff dough. Drop by spoonfuls onto oiled cookie sheet and push a pinch of Granola into center of each. Bake at 375° for eight minutes.

Walnut-Sesame Squares

2 eggs, separated	¼ t sea salt
⅔ c molasses	½ t cinnamon, ground
1 c walnuts, chopped	½ t nutmeg, ground
¾ c sesame seeds	2 t baking powder
¼ c whole-wheat flour	1 c Granola

Beat yolks till thick, then blend in the molasses. Mix the other ingredients (except the Granola and egg whites) and add them to the molasses mixture. Beat the egg whites till stiff, then fold these in. Oil a long baking pan, spread the Granola in it, and pour on the dough. Bake for 30 minutes at 350°. Slice into squares and serve warm.

Raisin Crunch Sesame Cookies

1¼ c honey	½ c raisins
½ c butter	¾ c sesame seeds
1 egg	1¼ c whole-wheat flour
1¼ c Granola	½ t nutmeg, ground

Blend honey, butter, and egg. Mix together Granola, raisins, and sesame seeds and then stir into the honey mixture. Sift the flour and nutmeg together and add the other ingredients. Drop this dough by spoonfuls onto an oiled baking sheet, flatten, and bake at 375° until browned.

Exotic Cookies

You are sure never to have tasted these before.

½ c honey	½ t cinnamon, ground
½ c tahini (sesame butter)	1½ c Granola
½ c walnuts, chopped	¼ c dates, pitted and chopped

Blend the honey and tahini. Add the nuts and cinnamon, then the Granola and dates. Drop by spoonfuls onto oiled baking sheet and bake at 350° for ten minutes.

CHAPTER 12

GRANOLA IN CAKES AND FROSTINGS, PIES AND SHELLS

The cake section includes a few old favorites—sponge-cake, cheesecake, coffeecake, fruitcake, and an old favorite that is adapted: carob cake. And, among the others, such delights as petit fours, tortes, and Chestnut, Carob, and Granola Pudding-Cake. Granola introduces more texture than cakes usually have, and fits in well because its makings are similar to cake ingredients.

The frostings all are delicious in themselves. Usually frostings are merely smooth, of course. But consider, for instance, how excellent an addition coconut is in German chocolate. Thus for Granola, too, in the recipes here, which include vanilla and carob, and cream cheese, peanut butter, and coffee.

After three fine pie shell recipes comes the pie filling section. Many ordinary shells are flavorless, or even slightly distasteful; with Granola as an ingredient, this problem does not exist.

The pie fillings offered are as untraditional as are the frostings, and as successful. Both carefully introduce Granola into types that people already love, in such a way that there is an extra attraction. Several fruit pie fillings are assembled here, and ones utilizing cream, sour cream, or yogurt, plus recipes for pecan and ice cream pies.

151

CAKES

Carob-Granola Cake

Try it with Crunchy Carob Frosting.

½ c butter
1⅔ c honey
2 eggs
½ c water
½ c carob powder
2½ c whole-wheat pastry
flour

½ t baking soda
½ t sea salt
⅓ c yogurt
⅓ c milk
½ c Granola

Cream butter and honey. Beat in eggs. Combine water and carob powder and stir into honey mixture. Sift flour, baking soda, and salt together twice. Add half of the flour mixture to the honey-carob mixture, then combine and add yogurt and milk. Stir in Granola and the remaining flour mixture. Pour into oiled 9- x 14-inch cake pan. Bake for 35 minutes at 350°.

Granola Spongecake

3 eggs
3 eggs, separated
1 c date sugar
⅛ t sea salt

1⅛ c whole-wheat flour
¾ c Granola, ground
¼ c Granola

Beat eggs and yolks with sugar and salt until thick. Beat egg whites to stiff peak, and fold in. Sift in flour and add ground and whole Granola. Fold briefly to blend. Pour into 9-inch loaf pan lined with wax paper. Bake at 375° for 30 minutes. Invert pan over rack. The wax paper will allow the cake to come out of the pan immediately. Remove the paper when cool.

Granola Cheesecake

2 eggs	¾ t almond extract
¾ c plus ⅓ c honey	1 c sour cream
16 oz. cream cheese	½ c Granola
¼ c powdered milk	pie shell
1 T vanilla extract	

Beat eggs, ¾ cup of the honey, cream cheese, powdered milk, 2 tsp. of the vanilla, and almond extract until smooth. Pour cheese mixture into 8-inch pan lined with pie shell. Set on low rack in a pan of boiling water and bake for 25 minutes at 300°. Stir together sour cream, Granola, 1 tsp. of vanilla, and ⅓ cup of the honey. When oven time is over, pour sweetened sour cream over top of cheesecake and return to oven for ten more minutes.

Granola Coffeecake

Use a coffee substitute if you prefer.

1½ c strong coffee	½ c raisins
1 t vanilla extract	½ c butter
1½ c date sugar	2 c whole-wheat pastry
1 t cinnamon, ground	flour
½ t cloves, ground	½ c Granola
¼ t sea salt	½ t baking soda

Combine all ingredients, except flour, Granola, and baking soda, in saucepan and boil for three minutes. Cool. Mix remaining ingredients and add to first mixture. Pour into oiled, floured pan and bake at 325° for 35 minutes.

Granola Fruitcake

2 c dates, pitted and chopped	½ c raisins
1 c figs, chopped	½ c shredded coconut
½ c dried apricots, chopped	½ c chopped walnuts
	2 c Granola

Mix all ingredients thoroughly. Press firmly into oiled loaf pan. Chill for four hours, and then turn onto plate.

Granola Brown Betty

¾ c Granola
3 T molasses
1 t cinnamon, ground
⅛ t sea salt
1 t lemon peel, ground

3 apples, cored and sliced
juice of ½ lemon
1 T butter

Mix Granola, molasses, cinnamon, salt, and lemon peel. In oiled 1½-quart baking dish, arrange in alternate layers of Granola mixture and apples. Sprinkle top with lemon juice and dot with butter. Bake for 30 minutes at 350°.

Granola Pumpkin Cake

⅔ c pumpkin, cooked and puréed
½ c Granola
½ c sour cream
¾ c molasses
⅓ c vegetable oil
3 eggs, beaten
1½ c whole-wheat flour

1 t ginger, ground
¼ t sea salt
½ t cinnamon, ground
½ t nutmeg, ground
½ t cloves, ground
½ t allspice, ground
¼ t mace, ground

Combine all ingredients. Turn into oiled 8- by 12-inch pan; bake at 350° for 50 minutes. Cool. Cut into squares.

Pineapple Torte with Nuts and Granola

5 eggs, separated
½ c honey
1½ c Granola, ground

3 c pecans, ground
3 c pineapple, crushed

Beat yolks until light, then beat in honey. Add Granola and nuts, and beat. Stir in pineapple. Beat egg whites stiffly and fold in. Bake for 30 minutes at 325° in a large oiled baking pan.

Carrot Granola Torte

6 eggs, separated	¼ c walnuts
⅔ c honey	1 c whole-wheat pastry
1 c carrots, grated	flour
¾ c Granola	1 t cinnamon, ground

Cream yolks and honey. Stir other ingredients in, except egg whites. Beat whites until stiff and fold in. Bake in 8-inch square glass pan for 45 minutes at 350°.

Chestnut, Carob, and Granola Pudding-Cake

1 lb chestnuts, shelled, cooked and mashed	⅓ c carob powder
½ c Granola	½ c honey
½ c butter	1 t vanilla extract

Mix together all the ingredients, while the chestnuts are still hot. Press into oiled bread pan lined with waxed paper. Cover and chill overnight. Unmold and peel off paper.

Maize Cake with Granola

4 eggs, separated	⅓ c maize flour
¼ c date sugar	¼ c Granola

Cream yolks and sugar to a smooth paste. Beat whites until thick. Add whites to yolks. Mix flour and Granola and stir slowly into egg mixture. Bake in oiled 9-inch baking pan for 15 minutes at 325°.

Granola-Carob Petits Fours

½ c carob powder	½ c dates, pitted and
2 T hot water	chopped
2 T honey	2 c Granola

Combine the carob powder, water, and honey over heat. Stir in the Granola, then dates. Shape into walnut-sized balls, and cool.

FROSTINGS

Vanilla-Granola Frosting

1 c honey	½ c Granola
½ c cream	1 c powdered milk
2 T butter	1 t vanilla extract

Combine honey, cream, and butter, and boil slowly for two minutes. Cool. Stir in Granola, powdered milk, and vanilla.

Crunchy Carob Frosting

⅓ c carob powder	¼ c milk
⅔ c powdered milk	1 t vanilla extract
¼ c honey	¼ c Granola
2 T vegetable oil	

Blend all ingredients except Granola in electric blender until smooth. Stir in Granola.

Maple-Granola Frosting

The maple syrup and date sugar together pack a wallop.

1 c maple syrup	2 T butter
¼ c date sugar	1 c powdered milk
½ c cream	½ c Granola

Combine syrup, sugar, cream, and butter. Boil softly for two minutes. Cool, then beat in the powdered milk and stir in the Granola.

Cream Cheese and Granola Frosting

8 oz cream cheese	1½ c date sugar
¼ lb butter	⅓ c Granola
¾ c honey	

Cream the cheese, butter, and honey. Beat in the sugar, then the Granola.

Peppermint and Granola Frosting

1 c honey	1 c powdered milk
½ c cream	1 t peppermint oil
2 T butter	½ c Granola

Combine honey, cream, and butter in saucepan. Slowly boil for two minutes. Cool. Beat in powdered milk and peppermint oil and fold in Granola.

Peanut Butter-Granola Frosting

½ c peanut butter	¼ c warm milk
2 T vegetable oil	¼ c Granola
½ c honey	

Whip all ingredients but Granola together, then fold in Granola.

Lemon Frosting with Granola

¾ c date sugar	2 T butter
½ c honey	1 c powdered milk
½ c cream	¼ c Granola
1 lemon, grated rind of	

Combine sugar, honey, cream, rind, and butter. Boil slowly for two minutes. Cool. Then beat in powdered milk and stir in Granola.

Crunchy Coffee Cream Frosting

Rich, creamy, and munchy. You might prefer to use a coffee substitute.

¼ c strong coffee	¼ c honey
¼ c butter	2 c whipping cream
¼ c powdered milk	1 c Granola

Cream the coffee, butter, powdered milk, and 2 Tbsp. of the honey. Whip the cream with the rest of the honey. Fold these two mixtures together and add the Granola.

PIE SHELLS

Granola Pastry for Two-Crust Pie

1 c sifted whole-wheat flour	½ t sea salt
¼ c Granola, ground	½ c vegetable oil
½ t baking powder	3 T cold water

Sift flour into mixing bowl. Add ground Granola, baking powder, and salt. Add the oil, and mix in with a fork. Sprinkle on the water and mix well. Form a ball, adding extra oil if the mixture is too dry. Divide in two and flatten each part into an 8- or 9-inch circle. Roll between sheets of wax paper.

Marla's Granola Pie Shell

Great for cheesecake and ice cream pie, among others.

1¼ c Granola	¼ c brown or date sugar
¼ c butter	¼ t nutmeg, ground

In a bowl combine Granola, sugar, nutmeg. Mix thoroughly. Blend in butter. Press mixture into a 9-inch pie pan. Chill until ready to use.

Ground Granola Pie Crust

1⅓ c Granola, ground	¼ t nutmeg, cinnamon, or
¼ c soft butter	other spice (optional)

Combine and mix with hands till the dough is crumbly. Press into a pie pan. Bake in a 375° oven for eight minutes. Refrigerate while you prepare the filling.

PIE FILLINGS

Crunchy Apple Pie Filling

An all-American favorite, updated with Granola.

¾ c Granola	1 t cinnamon, ground
⅓ c date sugar	⅛ t cloves, ground
3 T butter	2 c apple purée

Combine the Granola, date sugar, and butter in a saucepan, cook ten minutes, and cool for a few minutes. Mix the cinnamon and cloves into the apple purée. Combine the Granola and apple mixtures. In pie shell, bake 30 minutes at 350°.

Strawberry Pie Filling

3 T whole-wheat pastry flour	3½ c strawberries
⅔ c date sugar	½ c evaporated milk
⅛ t sea salt	¼ c powdered milk
¼ c Granola	1 T lemon juice

Combine flour, sugar, and salt in saucepan. Add Granola, then 1½ cups of the strawberries. Cook ten minutes and chill. Put 2 cups of the strawberries into 9-inch baked pie shell. Whip evaporated milk until stiff. Stir powdered milk and lemon juice in. Join milk mixture with cooked fruit. Pour over uncooked fruit in crust. Chill before serving.

Cherry Pie Filling

¾ c honey	⅛ t sea salt
3 T whole-wheat pastry flour	5½ c cherries, pitted
	¼ c Granola

Mix honey, flour, and salt in saucepan. Add 2½ cups cherries. Cook for ten minutes. Put remaining cherries in pie shell, cover with Granola, and pour cooked cherries over. Press top shell on. Bake at 325° for 35 minutes.

Blueberry Pie Filling

3 T whole-wheat pastry   ½ c evaporated milk
½ c honey   ¼ c powdered milk
⅛ t sea salt   ¼ c Granola, ground
3½ c blueberries

Mix flour, honey, and salt in saucepan. Add 1½ cups of the blueberries. Cook ten minutes, stirring to crush blueberries, then chill. Put 2 cups blueberries into a baked 9-inch pie shell. Whip evaporated milk until stiff and stir in powdered milk and Granola. Combine milk mixture with cooked fruit. Pour over uncooked fruit in crust. Chill until served.

Granola Pecan Pie Filling

2   eggs   ½ t vanilla extract
¾ c molasses   ¼ c Granola
2 T butter   1½ c pecan pieces

Beat the eggs a couple of minutes, then add the molasses, butter, and vanilla. Stir in the Granola and pecans. Pour into pastry-lined pie plate and bake for 45 minutes at 375°.

Lemon Cream Pie Filling

4   eggs   2   lemons
¾ c honey   4 T butter
¼ c Granola, ground   1 c whipping cream

Beat eggs and honey in the top part of a double boiler. Stir in the Granola, then the rind of one lemon, juice of both lemons, and butter. Cook over hot water, stirring constantly, until thick. Remove from heat and cool to lukewarm. Fold into shell. Whip cream until stiff and spread over lemon mixture. Chill.

Coconut-Banana-Granola Meringue Pie Filling

4 bananas, peeled	½ c Granola
1 t lemon juice	4 egg whites
1 c shredded coconut	⅓ c date sugar

Mash bananas and add lemon juice, then coconut and Granola. Spoon into crust. Beat egg whites and date sugar into meringue, and cover pie. Bake at 350° until meringue begins to brown.

Sour Cream Raisin Pie Filling

2 eggs	1 t cinnamon, ground
1 c sour cream	1 c raisins
¾ c honey	1 c Granola
½ t cloves, ground	

Beat together the eggs, sour cream, honey, cloves, and cinnamon. Stir in the raisins and Granola. Pour into 9-inch pie shell and bake at 350° for 45 minutes.

Granola Yogurt Pie Filling

1 c yogurt	1 t vanilla extract
1 c cottage cheese	1 c Granola
1 T honey	

Whip together all ingredients except Granola, then fold that in. Fill 8-inch baked pie shell. Refrigerate a few hours.

Ice Cream Pie Filling

2½ c ice cream	1½ c Granola

Combine. Pack into cooked pie shell and freeze.

Whole-Wheat Granola Tart Filling

½ c raisins
½ c dried currants
¼ c figs, chopped
 2 T water

2 t whole-wheat pastry
      flour
1 T vegetable oil
½ c Granola
½ c orange juice

Over low heat, cook fruits and water for 20 minutes. Stir in flour and cook ten minutes more. Remove from heat. Stir in oil, Granola, and orange juice. When cool, spoon into 18 tart shells made from pie pastry, and bake at 450° for 15 minutes.

CHAPTER 13

GRANOLA CANDY AND OTHER SWEET TREATS

Granola seems relatively foreign to candy. Nevertheless, it is certainly appropriate to substitute Granola for nuts, or to use it as a coating, and it serves these functions well with candies. We have, in fact, found no difficulty in blending Granola into creams, fudge, divinity, popcorn balls, fondant, brittle, and so on.

In the More Sweet Treats section, you will find "the ones that almost got away," that evaded our categories and that just had to be included. There is a pudding, for instance, and sweet potato puffs. Not to mention a milkshake and four different kinds of ice cream. All benefiting from Granola.

Enjoy.

CANDIES

Granola Creams

½ c honey
½ c sweetened condensed
    milk
2 T butter

2 T Granola
¾ c powdered milk
extra Granola

Heat honey, milk, and butter in top of double boiler, over boiling water, for ten minutes. Remove from heat, cool, and stir in 2 Tbsp. Granola and the powdered milk. Drop from teaspoon onto aluminum foil. Put a bit of extra Granola on top of each cream.

Granola Divinity

3 T water	1 T vanilla extract
1 t vinegar	1 c Granola
1 c honey	1¼ c powdered milk
1 egg white	

Stir together the water, vinegar, and honey. Bring to boil and boil for two minutes. Beat egg white until stiff. Pour boiling syrup over egg white and beat a couple of minutes. Cool, then add vanilla, Granola, and powdered milk. Push from teaspoon onto aluminum foil. Cool at least an hour.

Granola Carob Fudge
A really fine fudge.

⅔ c carob powder	¼ c shredded coconut
1½ c powdered milk	¼ c honey
1 c Granola	⅓ stick butter
1 c peanut butter	1 t vanilla extract
1 c date sugar	½ c milk

Mix all ingredients thoroughly. Spread evenly on a flat board or pan and refrigerate until firm enough to cut. Cut into squares and separate. Leave in open air several hours until firm enough to handle easily.

Carob-Milk Candies with Granola
A Granola with lots of nuts makes it twice as good.

1 c Granola	¼ c honey
1 c powdered milk	¼ c oil
¼ c carob powder	

Combine the Granola, powdered milk, and carob powder thoroughly. Stirring, heat the honey and oil in a saucepan over a moderate heat briefly until they are combined and easy to pour. Add the oil-honey liquid into the dry ingredients, and stir until mixed. With your hands, form this candy into walnut-sized pieces. Place in the refrigerator 30 minutes or more to firm.

Granola Brittle

2 c date sugar   1 c Granola

Heat sugar in heavy frypan over moderate heat, stirring constantly, until sugar becomes a brown syrup. Add the Granola. Pour onto a cold, oiled platter. When cold and hard, break into pieces.

Granola-Fondant Balls

¼ c mashed potatoes   1 c date sugar
2 T butter   ½ c powdered milk
1 t almond extract   3 c Granola, ground

Add hot potatoes, butter, almond extract, and stir well. Sift sugar and milk together and stir in. Chill. Shape into balls and roll in Granola.

Pineapple-Granola Kisses

2 T butter   ½ c Granola
1 c date sugar   ¾ c powdered milk
½ c crushed pineapple

Boil butter, sugar, and pineapple slowly for two minutes, until sugar is melted. Cool and stir in Granola and powdered milk until candy is smooth. Drop from teaspoon onto buttered waxed paper. Chill at least an hour.

Jane's Peanut Butter Fudge Balls

Our favorite confection. Rich and nutritious.

½ c peanut butter	2 T Granola
⅓ c powdered milk	½ T honey

Mix thoroughly in bowl. Shape into walnut-sized balls. Refrigerate for best flavor. Variations: Use tiger's milk powder instead of powdered milk. Roll balls in carob powder or additional Granola before refrigerating.

Peanut Butter Jewels

1 c peanut butter	1 t vanilla extract
½ c maple syrup	1½ c shredded coconut
1 c Granola	

Mix peanut butter with syrup, Granola, and vanilla. Spread coconut on wax paper. Drop spoonfuls of peanut mixture onto coconut and roll to coat. Chill.

Peanut Butter and Granola Log

½ c peanut butter	½ c Granola
⅓ c powdered milk	2 T honey
½ c shredded coconut	

Mix peanut butter and powdered milk. Spread coconut evenly on waxed paper. Press peanut butter mixture over the coconut thinly to make a square, the underside of which is covered with coconut. Mix the honey and Granola and spread evenly on topside of peanut butter. Roll rectangle up and seal by pinching. Chill and slice.

Sesame Granola Candy

1⅔ c sesame seeds, roasted
  and ground
⅓ c Granola
1 T sesame oil
¼ c honey

2 T butter
1 t vanilla extract
½ t cinnamon, ground
¼ t cloves, ground
¼ t mace, ground

Mix all ingredients and shape into wafers.

Sesame Granola Pudding-Candy

¼ c cornstarch
1¼ c water
¼ c tahini (sesame butter)

¼ c honey
⅓ c Granola

Dissolve the cornstarch in ½ cup of the water. Heat the tahini, honey, and remaining water gently in a saucepan until totally blended. Then bring to a boil. Pour in dissolved cornstarch, stirring. When thickened, lower heat and cook for 20 minutes while stirring. Then mix Granola in and pour into a pan. Chill.

Russian Confection

⅔ c cream cheese
⅓ c sour cream
½ c raisins
½ c butter
½ c honey

½ c Granola
2 T dates, pitted
  and chopped
2 T grated orange rind

Combine all ingredients and press 1-inch thick into oiled pan. Chill overnight.

Granola Cheese Balls

¾ c dates, pitted and
  chopped
1 T whole-wheat flour
½ c shredded coconut

1 T grated lemon rind
½ t allspice, ground
1 lb cream cheese
¾ c Granola, ground

Mix dates with a little of the whole-wheat flour. Mix dates, coconut, rind, allspice, and remaining flour, then blend into cheese. Shape into 1-inch balls, and roll in Granola to coat.

Granola Popcorn Balls

1 c honey	8 c popped corn
¼ c water	2 c Granola
1 t vanilla extract	

Stir honey and water over high heat until it boils. Reduce heat and continue stirring. When a bit of the mixture will form a ball in cold water, remove pan from heat. Mix in vanilla, pour over popcorn, and form balls. Roll in the Granola, to coat. Allow to cool.

MORE SWEET TREATS

Sweet, Spicy Granola

1 egg white, beaten slightly	1 t cinnamon, ground
	1 t ginger, ground
1 c Granola	⅛ t allspice, ground
¼ c date sugar	⅛ t nutmeg, ground

Pour egg white over Granola and stir. Mix sugar and spices, and sprinkle over the Granola. Spread onto an oiled baking sheet and bake for 25 minutes at 300°. Cool.

Vanilla-Granola Pudding

⅓ c date sugar	1 T vanilla extract
1½ T cornstarch	3 T butter
¼ t sea salt	1 c Granola
1⅔ c boiling water	

Combine date sugar, cornstarch, and salt in saucepan and add water slowly, stirring constantly. Cook over medium heat, continuing to stir, until mixture is thick and clear; then cook three more minutes. Off the heat, stir in the vanilla, butter, and Granola.

Pineapple Granola Dips

1	pineapple, cut into 2-in square slices	1 c	honey
		1 c	Granola

Stick a toothpick into each piece of pineapple, dip the pieces in the honey, and roll them in Granola. Refrigerate before serving.

Sweet Potato and Granola Puffs

2 c	sweet potatoes, cooked, mashed and chilled	¼ t	cloves, ground
		¼ t	cinnamon, ground
2	eggs, beaten	¼ t	nutmeg, ground
⅔ c	whole-wheat flour	½ c	Granola
1½ t	baking powder		vegetable oil
½ t	sea salt	⅔ c	date sugar

Mix potatoes and eggs. Sift flour, baking powder, and spices together and combine with potato mixture and Granola. Roll out ½ inch thick and cut into squares. Deep-fry in oil for three minutes. Drain and sprinkle with date sugar.

Granola Milkshake

¼ c	Granola, ground	¼ c	vanilla ice cream
1 c	cold milk		

Soak Granola in milk for ten minutes. Add ice cream, and beat (or blend in electric blender) until smooth.

Carob-Granola Ice Cream

1½ c sweetened evaporated   3 T carob powder
      milk   ½ c Granola
¼ c honey

Combine milk, honey, and carob powder in an electric blender. Pour into an ice cube tray (without the cube rack) and freeze for two hours. Press Granola into top and continue freezing until very firm.

Fruit and Granola Ice Cream

1⅓ c orange juice   ½ c strawberries, sliced
¾ c powdered milk   ¼ c Granola

Whip juice and powdered milk together and pour into ice cube tray (without cube rack). Freeze for one hour, then stir in strawberries and Granola. Freeze overnight.

Peanut Butter Ice Cream with Granola

1½ c sweetened evaporated   ¼ c peanut butter
      milk   ½ c Granola
¼ c honey

Blend milk, honey, and peanut butter in electric blender. Pour into ice cube tray (without cube rack) and freeze for one hour. Stir Granola in. Freeze overnight.

Granola Ice Cream

¾ c honey   2 c heavy cream,
4   eggs, separated   whipped
1 t vanilla extract   1 c Granola

Beat honey, egg yolks, and vanilla until creamy. Mix in cream and Granola. Beat egg whites stiffly and fold in. Freeze in ice cube tray without cube rack.

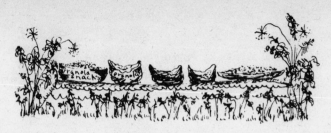

CHAPTER 14

PARTY SNACKS AND GRANOLA

This chapter could contain many of the recipes in the chapters that have come before. The foods that can serve so well as party snacks are really first and foremost other dishes and belong in other chapters.

Granolas themselves, for example, make really fantastic party treats. Check out Chapters 1 and 2 for yourself and see. Even the basic Granolas do well. And besides them, think about Maple Syrup, Nutty Special, Sweet-and-Sour, Chili-Flavored, Garlic, Wispy Mint, Curried, or Fruity Granola. Snacker's delights, each one.

And don't let the Granola sweets get by you. The cookies and candies chapters (11 and 13) especially offer many perfect possibilities.

Perhaps sweetness isn't what you are seeking. Try the vegetable chapter (5). There you will find Zucchini-Granola Patties (you could make little ones), Granola in Grape Leaves, and Granola Okra Fries. Or take a look at Chapter 6, the egg chapter. Granola Egg Fondue would make a stunning party event, and there are Granola-Stuffed Eggs, and Healthy Eggnog. The Breads and Spreads chapter (10), is a natural, too.

Fruit also is appropriate for party eating. We refer you to Chapters 8 and 9, where fruits and salads are considered. The salad chapter includes many recipes for fruit salads. And in the fruit chapter are such pleasures as Granola Banana Bites, Granola Spiced Fruit, Stuffed Figs, and Fried Banana-Granola.

Now that we have directed you elsewhere, we will conclude with a few recipes that do, after all, fit better here than there.

Garbanzo Granola Snacks

2 T butter
2 garlic cloves, crushed
1 c garbanzo beans, cooked
1 c sesame seeds

½ c Granola
½ t ginger, ground
¼ t dry mustard
1 t sea salt

In the butter, sauté the garlic, then add the cooked garbanzo beans, stirring often, until beans are golden brown. Mix into the sesame seeds and Granola, and stir in the seasonings.

Fried Parmesan Bites

2 egg whites
¼ t sea salt
⅛ t ground pepper

3 oz Parmesan cheese, grated
1 T Granola
vegetable oil

Beat egg whites until stiff. Stir in salt and pepper, then cheese and Granola. Drop by teaspoonfuls into hot deep oil and cook until lightly brown. Drain on paper towels.

Granola and Soy Nuts

1 c dried soybeans, soaked overnight in water
1 T sea salt
2 c Granola

Drain soybeans and spread into oiled skillet over moderate heat. Stir regularly. Cook until crisp and lightly brown, about an hour; they will resemble Spanish peanuts in appearance. Sprinkle with salt. Stir into Granola.

Curried Granola Nuts

1 c almonds, chopped   ¼ c butter
    coarsely   2 t curry powder
1 c Granola

Sauté nuts and Granola in butter for ten minutes, stirring often. Sprinkle curry powder in and continue cooking and stirring for six more minutes. Drain on paper towels.

Garlic Granola Nuts

2   garlic cloves, minced   1 c cashew pieces
¼ c butter   1 c Granola
¼ t ground pepper   1 T tamari

Sauté garlic in butter. Add pepper, nuts, and Granola and cook for 15 minutes, stirring often. Stir tamari in. Drain on paper towels.

INDEX

Bagels, 133
Breads
  Non–yeast, 126–129
    African Banana Loaf,
      128–129
    Boston Brown Bread, 126
    Cornbread, 127
    Crunchy Bread, 128
    Date Bread, 127
    Heavy Loaf, 127
    Naomi's Hobo Bread,
      128
    Orange Marmalade
      Bread, 129
  Rolls, etc., 129–135
    Bagels, Egg, 133
    Buns, Whole–Wheat, 130
    Chewy Meal Patties, 135
    Crackers, Sesame, 134
    Croquettes, 134
    Date Gems, 132
    Doughnuts, Whole–
      Wheat, 135
    Dumplings, 73
    Indian Fried Bread, 134
    Muffins, 131–132
    Pancakes, 46–47
    Pizza Dough, Whole–
      Wheat, 133
    Rolls, 129–130
    Sticks, 132

Breakfast Ideas, 42–44, 47
  Adding to the bowl, 43–44
  Blending in, 43
  Cantaloupe as bowl, 44
  Ground Granola, 43–44
  Mixed with store cereal, 44
  Soaked or dry, 43
  see also 47
Breakfast Ideas for Children,
  47–49
Breakfast Recipes, 44–47
  Apple Breakfast, 44
  Breakfast Salad, 45
  Figs with a Carrot, 46
  Fruit and Cream, 45–46
  Grapefruit, 45
  Millet, 45
  Pancakes, 46–47

Cake Frostings, 156–157
  Cream Cheese, 156
  Crunchy Carob, 156
  Crunchy Coffee Cream, 157
  Lemon, 157
  Maple, 156
  Peanut Butter, 157
  Peppermint, 157
  Vanilla, 156
Cakes, 151–155
  Brown Betty, 154
  Carob, 152

175

178   INDEX